MISSION POSSIBLE:
How to Graduate from College Debt-Free

_____

Presented To:

_____

Presented By:

_____

Date:

_____

MISSION POSSIBLE: How to Graduate from College Debt-Free

By

Dr. Juan Phillip Chisholm

Green Light Books & Publishing, LLC
P.O. Box 1965
Orlando, Florida 32802-1965
www.GreenlightBooks.org
Book Orders: Info@greenlightbooks.org

www.GraduateDebtFreeClub.com
www.Investitude.com
www.YoungInvestors.org
www.JuanChisholm.com

Published by Juan Phillip Chisholm

ISBN: 978-0-9755110-4-6

LEGAL NOTICE: This publication is designed to provide competent and reliable information regarding the subject covered. However, it is sold with the understanding that the author and publisher are not engaged in rendering legal, financial, or other professional advice. Laws and practices often vary from state to state and if legal or other expert assistance is required, the services of a professional practitioner should be sought. The author and publisher specifically disclaim any liability that is incurred from the use or application of the contents herein.

Investitude™ is a registered trademark of Juan Phillip Chisholm.

MISSION POSSIBLE: How to Graduate from College Debt-Free

By

Dr. Juan Phillip Chisholm

Dedication

In loving memory of Mr. Eugene & Mrs. Alnora Rebecca Chisholm:

Thank you dad and mom for believing in me, teaching me the power of positive self-esteem, always trusting me to do what's best, and sharing so many impactful lessons with me that I continue to grow from and share with so many others.

You are and will continue to be forever in my heart as I continue the legacy that you shared with me.

- JPC

About the Author

Dr. Juan P. Chisholm is an acclaimed business owner, teacher, investor, author, and motivational speaker. He has successfully completed the world-renown Executive Education program in Strategic Finance at the Harvard Business School in Boston. He is the published author of three (3) financial books:

#1: *How to Make Your Past, A Blessing to Your Future* (www.Greenlightbooks.org);

#2: *Investitude* (www.Investitiude.com); and

#3: *Mission Possible: How to Graduate from College Debt-Free* (www.GraduateDebtFreeClub.com).

Also, Dr. Chisholm was featured in an exclusive interview in Black Enterprise® Magazine, the premiere wealth-building resource for African Americans on ways to graduate from college debt-free. He is also the Founder of Young Investors, Inc., a non-profit that educates high-school students, college students, and young adults regarding financial literacy and investment strategies. Learn more about Young Investors, Inc. at www.YoungInvestors.org.

Dr. Juan P. Chisholm is also a proud graduate of Florida State University (FSU). While attending FSU, he majored in English Literature and minored in Business, Economics and Black Studies. He was elected FSU's Homecoming King and was also selected as Florida's College Brother of the Year Award of Alpha Phi Alpha Fraternity, Inc. After graduating from Florida State University, he earned his law degree from Florida A&M University College of Law in Orlando, Florida where he was the two-time recipient of the prestigious Percy R. Luney Spirit of Service Award.

Dr. Juan P. Chisholm is active in the community. He serves on the Board of Directors of Revolution Leadership®, Inc. (www.RevolutionLeadership.org), a national non-profit organization that awards college scholarships and serves students nationwide. He is active in his local church and is the founder of American Nation Builders College Preparatory Academy (www.AmericanNationBuilders.org).

Dr. Juan P. Chisholm is happily married to his wife and best-friend, Attorney Audrey K. Chisholm. They reside in the beautiful city of Orlando, Florida and are parents of three beautiful daughters and one son.

www.JuanChisholm.com

Acknowledgements

I thank you God for being my guiding light and inspiration. Without you Lord, this seed would not be planted.

Also, I thank you for the wonderful and loving friend that you have given me through my wife Audrey. I now understand what it means and feels like to have my other half make me feel complete. Thank you for all of your love, help, support and patience as your author was finding his inspiration for Investitude. I love you.

To my grandmother, I love you. Thank you for being my biggest fan and most loyal supporter. Also, thank you for always telling me how proud you are. Your affirmation and love means a great deal.

Mom and Dad, thank you for always being so supportive of me and reminding me to take care of business. Thank you for your love, support, and prayers.

To my second mom and dad (and Ms. Turner), thank you for making me laugh and welcoming me inside your hearts. Also, thank you for having reared up such a strong and wonderful woman of God to call my wife. I love and appreciate all of you. To Carlos,

Jason, James, Carlos II, Jade, Alice, and Amanda – you all are loved very much.

Lastly, to my friends, extended family and readers, thank you for sharing another adventure with me. Also, thank you all for helping send me to Harvard. I hope you find this one is even more interesting than the first. And a special thank you to my friends, Tarsha Thomas, Marcus Johnson and Ms. Delia Winston for all of your love and prayers.

I thank you again God for opening my eyes to brighter days. And to the readers of this book, I pray that these chapters of my life will be a blessing unto you.

Love,

Juan

Foreword

When God gave me the vision to write, *Investitude*, he told me that "It is time to become, who you are destined to be." I excitedly scribbled this phrase down on the first sheet of paper I could find. Then, as I was led to *glance* at that paper again, after again, and after again, I became irritated and doubtful because I realized that at that moment in my life, I felt that achieving this vision would be impossible because I had been caught in the middle of a spiritual storm. But, that's when the Holy Spirit would constantly re-affirm me through the Lord's life-breathing *words* of affirmation that "It is time to become, who I am destined to be."

I trusted God's Words for my life and pressed towards the mark despite my flesh and was delivered from my storm. There, I was able to rest and in a place of peace; everything remaining from the storm was now Beautiful, and I was able to appreciate the Lord's faithfulness and what He had carried me through.

Through that particular testimony in my life, I believe that it all had to happen in order to unlock blessings for my family members, friends, and students; and successfully bring unbelievers to Christ. God also used that testimony to channel me in a new career. I re-entered school to pursue a J.D., purchased a new home, and I am now married to my lovely wife, Mrs. Audrey K. Chisholm, J.D. What I learned from this experience is to continue to trust God in the mist of the storms of your life, for His direction and through His direction, God revealed that you become who you are destined to be. I pray that this nugget from my life helps you to reaching your potential/promised land and encourages you to believe that your time is here and "It's time to become, who you are destined to be."

Table of Contents

Unit One: Mission Possible:
You Can Graduate From College Debt-Free

Unit Two: Mission Possible: Always include the Required
Basic Ingredients and Scholarship Non-Negotiables

Unit Three: Finding Money for College Tuition

Unit Four: Mission Possible: Covering the Cost of College Housing

Unit Five: Mission Possible: Covering the Cost of Books

Unit Six: Mission Possible: Other Ways To Pay For College (Tuition, Housing, & Books)

Unit Seven: Mission Possible: You Now Have the Tools to Graduate From College Debt-Free

MISSION POSSIBLE:
How to Graduate from College Debt-Free

Unit One:
Mission Possible:
You can Graduate From
College Debt-Free

Chapter I

Mission Possible:
How to Graduate From
College Debt-Free?

Mission Possible: How to Graduate From College Debt-Free

"No one can go back and make a brand-new start, my friend, but anyone can start from here and make a brand-new end."

Anonymous

Home: Heart, Mind, and Soul.
Please, Park Here First.

Mission Possible: How to Graduate from College Debt-Free, in a nutshell teaches you how to graduate from college without any school loans or debt.

This is achieved by showing you practical strategies and techniques as well as sharing information that will help you to find scholarships, awards, and other beneficial opportunities that will help you to pay for college education and its associated expenses (college tuition, housing, and books) without taking out a school loan. Additionally, in Mission Possible: How to Graduate From College Debt-Free, I share my college experience and the specific *Basic Ingredients* (See Unit Two) that I implemented to graduate from Florida State University, the Florida Agricultural & Mechanical University's (FAMU's) College of Law, and complete an Executive Education Program in Strategic Finance for Smaller Businesses from the Harvard Business School all debt-free.

In addition, I will share my personal tools for success in Unit II (which is a Unit you do not want to skip) that will increase your chances of earning scholarships, awards, and other beneficial opportunities that will maximize your chances of graduating from college debt-free. I will also address some of the negative associated stereotypes and stigmas that hold so many people back from reaching their full potential in Chapter 5. *Yep, Chapter 5 will address some of that scary mental stuff that we all wrestle with that holds us back from achieving our dreams, goals, and aspirations.* It is definitely a must-read chapter that is designed to help you to get outside of your mind and go beyond what you thought was impossible to achieve.

Other chapters of Mission Possible, How to Graduate From College Debt-Free, will also share impactful material on equipping you with the right tools of success such as having a winning attitude and on positive thinking (see chapter 3). These chapters will encourage you to appreciate how your success is directly tied to the way you think of yourself and see yourself. This will also serve as an important part of your reading because it will serve as an important building block in our later discussion in chapter 3 concerning the right attitude to have when overcoming the hurdles of a low GPA or SAT/ACT when applying for a grade sensitive scholarship, award, or beneficial opportunity.

Is this book for me?

Mission Possible: How to Graduate from College Debt-Free is aimed at any motivated person that is interested in learning more about finding money to pay for college. The groups that may mostly benefit from this material includes motivated parents of students interested in attending college as well as motivated students that are actually interested in college or already attending college. Additionally, a motivated student that is either in high-school, middle-school, or elementary school that is thinking ahead about their future college plans would likely benefit greatly from this material.

The other factor to consider is time. The person that has more time will have more opportunities to implement the strategies shared in this book. Ideally, if pursuing scholarships in this book and learning more about the material could be treated as a part-time job (with an eighteen to twenty-hour weekly commitment to work towards your scholarship goals), then I believe you will be well on your way to earning a plethora of well-deserved scholarships.

So, let's get started on this journey of graduating from college debt-free.

Share your debt-free journey with us at
www.GraduateDebtFreeClub.com

Please, be sure to share your debt free journey with us online via our website: *www.GraduateDebtFreeClub.com* so that others can learn from your story as we expand the debt free community around the world, thereby encouraging others that it is possible to graduate from college debt-free.

Also, *www.GraduateDebtClubFree.com* is a free tool that allows you to learn more about other scholarship opportunities as well as receive prizes, awards, and points. We look forward to connecting with you soon.

Chapter II

How to Make my Graduate Debt-Free Plan and Track Its Success

How to Make my Graduate Debt Free Plan and Track Its Success

"Knowledge is like a garden: if it is not cultivated, it cannot be harvested."

African Proverb

Do you like strategy games? I know I do. The best ones for me are games like Checkers and Chess that involve strategies, board dynamics, and rules agreed upon that can help a person to win. Indeed, if you are not a fan of these games, then sitting across from a competitor either in person or online could be a bit intimidating. But this is also one of the most amazing aspects of a strategy game, as people can be taught how to improve their strategies by watching others and learning their tactics. Of course, this may make you more of a student of the game instead of being just a player of the game. Moreover, as you learn more, the game and its strategies may gradually become easier to understand, easier to follow, and easier to execute.

Although this learning aspect is what I enjoy most from a strategy game, it is also what I strive to do in *Mission Possible: How to Graduate from College Debt-Free*. Through the course of this book, the goal is to share real insight and strategies that have helped me and many others to graduate debt-free that you too can apply to your own life or situation in hope that you will have a similar outcome.

In time and in practice, I hope the recommendations I share will become norms that you routinely do that will make this process gradually easier for you because it will be easy to understand, easy to follow, and easy to execute.

Now, here are three (3) important strategies I would like you to routinely practice while reading this book, and in your pursuit of scholarships, awards, and other beneficial opportunities.

Three (3) Important Strategies for you to Follow that Should Become Routine Norms

These three strategies will help you to pay for college education and its associated expenses (college tuition, housing, and books).

The three strategies include 1) understanding the *Mission Possible: How to Graduate Debt-Free* reading rules; 2) Making your college debt-free plan of action; 3) constantly journaling your progress in your *Mission Possible: "I am Possible" Personal Accountability Reflection Notebook*.

I am hopeful that you will start using these three important strategies each time you read this book and apply for scholarships, awards, and other beneficial opportunities. I include additional details below.

Strategy#1: Understanding the Mission Possible: How to Graduate Debt-Free **Reading Rules**

First let's discuss what makes reading this book easy to understand, easy to follow, and easy to read. Here, I included seven (7) reading rules to assist you to easily read, *Mission Possible: How to Graduate Debt-Free*.

Seven (7) Reading Rules for *Mission Possible: How to Graduate from College Debt Free*

The following rules are designed to help guide your reading experience. I hope these rules are able to add to your reading by making it fun, easy, and interactive. Please, adhere to these rules while reading *Mission Possible: How to Graduate Debt-Free* below.

Rule #1: Name your book!

Return to the front pages of the book and give your *Mission Possible: How to Graduate from College Debt-Free* book a reputable name. This helps to establish a connection between you and your personal mission to graduate from college-debt-free, so we can work together to make it possible.

Rule #2: Feel free to write in the book as you read and learn more.

Feel free to write in the book as you read and learn more. This writing may also include *underlining, highlighting, circling, and all other types of markings*. The goal in asking that you write in your Mission Possible book is to provide you with all necessary means and tools to help you succeed and use this book as a true resource to achieve your goals. So, let's make it easy, feel free to write in your book.

Rule #3: Use your license to jump or power drive.

Through the course of your reading, rule # 3 gives you the option to either *jump* (skip around) or *power-drive* (read straight through). Therefore, if you choose to power-drive, you are reading Mission Possible in a linear direction (i.e. chapters 1, 2, 3...29) or you may choose to jump, which means that you have decided to read by *skipping around* (i.e. move from chapter one up to chapter twenty-three, then move *back* to chapter seven and finally return back to chapter one).

It is also okay if you randomly jump some chapters and power-drive others. Please, take advantage of the method that works best for you.

Also, if you do decide to jump around, you may find the Table of Contents helpful in directing you to the chapter that you want to land. Please, reference the Table of Contents for the specific page and chapters to where you would like to land.

Rule #4: Join our Graduate from College Debt-Free Club by visiting *www.GraduateDebtFreeClub.com*

Take advantage of all the resources available at *www.GraduateDebtFreeClub.com*. This website is designed to provide you with valuable tools of success, basic ingredients, and other resources that will help you to achieve your goals of going to college and graduating debt-free. Please, put these free resources to work by using them and recommending them to your friends and others. Feel free to share your debt-free journey on our website. Learn more at *www.GraduateDebtFreeClub.com*.

Rule #5: Share Mission Possible book and lessons with others.

Share Mission Possible and what you've learned with others. If you liked the concepts or enjoyed the materials, please, feel free to share it with your family members, church members, friends, colleagues, fellow classmates, and other people that you believe will truly benefit from this material.

Also, note that Mission Possible will also make a great gift for birthdays, graduations, and weddings. So, please, continue to share Mission Possible and the impactful lessons that you learn from it with others. For more information on purchasing a book for someone else, please visit one of the following websites to purchase a book directly from us:

- o *www.GraduateDebtFreeClub.com*
- o *www.YoungInvestors.org*
- o *www.JuanChisholm.com*
- o *www.Investitude.com*

Rule #6: Use the glossary.

Various terms are included throughout the text and can be looked up in the glossary at the end of the text. All of the words in bold lettering are defined via this glossary as well as a few others that are generally common to the subject matter of *Mission Possible: How to Graduate Debt-Free*. The glossary can be found at the end of the book. If you need more assistance in finding a term that is not in the glossary, please visit our web site for more resources and additional information.

Rule #7: Use the Mission Possible Hashtags

After posting about *Mission Possible: How to Graduate Debt-Free* on social media, please use our hashtags below:

#GraduateDebtFreeClub
#MissionPossibleDebtFree
#Investitude
#MissionPossibleGDF

It is our goal to create a conversation about the possibility of graduating from any college debt-free that can be discussed around the world through the power of the internet and social media.

Thank you for being a participant in this important conversation.

I hope you are able to apply these seven (7) rules while reading this book. They will help guide your reading and make it a more rewarding experience that is easy to follow, easy to understand, and easy to execute. Enjoy!

Mission Possible: Plan of Action

Next, it's important that we discuss making your **Mission Possible: Plan of Action**. This plan of action will keep you on track by making sure you have a plan that is easy to follow, easy to understand, and easy to execute. Please, complete the worksheet below to establish your plan of action. Please, ensure you write your responses inside your personal copy of Mission Possible: How to Graduate Debt-Free book.

<u>Mission Possible: Plan of Action</u>

Directions: Set your plan into action by answering the questions listed below.

I plan to graduate college from

_____

Name of College/University

I believe it will take me _____ years

# of years (i.e., AA = 2 years; BA/BS = 4 Years; MS = 5 or 6

to   graduate   with   a   degree   in

_____.

Specific Desired Degree or Major

This will cost a total of_____

Research the Total Cost for College at Your College of Choice

over the course of _____ years.

Total # of Years You Plan to be in College

Divide cost of college by _____.

Total # of Years You Plan to be in College

To graduate debt-free, I will need to find the following amount each year:

$_____ for Year #1

$_____ for Year #2

$_____ for Year #3

$_____ for Year #4

$_____ for Year #5

$_____ for Year #6

Now that we know how much you will need for each year of college, it is important that we establish a norm that will assist you to gauge your success during this process.

How do I gauge success with *"Mission Possible: How to Graduate from College Debt-Free?"*

As a word to the wise, I gauge success with Mission Possible based on the following *Mission Possible Accountability Reflection Questions* shared below.

Mission Possible Accountability Reflection Questions

1. How many scholarships did you apply for this week?
   a. Under twenty (20)?
   b. Between twenty-one (21) to forty-five (45).
   c. **Mission Possible sweet-spot**: Between forty-six (46) to fifty (50).
   d. Between fifty-one (51) to one hundred (100). How many? _____

2. Did you give it your best shot? *Yes or* no? How would you grade your overall application for this week? *A, B, C, D, & F?*

3. And why did you select this grade for yourself? Please, explain your rationale.

_____

_____

_____

4. Did you include the basic ingredients from the tools of success (see unit 2 to learn more) with every scholarship, award, or beneficial opportunity application:

    a. An updated resume – Y*es or No;*
    b. Four (4) letters of recommendation – Y*es or No;*
    c. A personal statement that turns your personal adversity into something good – *Yes or No;*
    d. A financial letter – *Yes or No*

5. Did you follow-up with the organizations or committees to check on your status? *Yes or No.*

6. Did you mail a thank you card (even if you did not receive the award)? *Yes or No.*

7. What did you learn from this week's experience?

_____

_____

I believe success is something that can be gradually achieved, instead of being done overnight.

As such, I gauge success from week to week based on a weekly or monthly reflection in which I answer and review my responses to the aforementioned six (6) **Mission Possible Accountability Reflection Questions.**

Also, please, purchase the *"I am Possible" Graduate Debt-Free Notebook* as a complimentary book to help track your scholarships, keep you on track with searching and applying for scholarships, and to keep you accountable in your scholarship pursuit over a twenty-four month period.

Please, visit one of the following websites to purchase the complimentary notebook:

www.GraduateDebtFreeClub.com
www.YoungInvestors.org
www.JuanChisholm.com
www.Investitude.com

Mission Possible Weekly Accountability Questions

The six (6) **Mission Possible Accountability Reflection Questions** are answered and reviewed every-week that you are able to mail out a batch of scholarship applications, awards, or other beneficial financial opportunities. These questions are designed to keep you accountable and to sharpen your skills, which increases your chances of earning scholarships, awards, and other beneficial opportunities.

Additionally, the **Mission Possible Accountability Reflection Questions and** *"I am Possible"* **Graduate Debt-Free Notebook** will help you to gauge your success with *Mission Possible: How to Graduate from College Debt-Free* and keep you on track.

Please, note that additional copies of the **Mission Possible Accountability Reflection Questions** are included in the appendix as well as the "I am Possible" Graduate Debt-Free Notebook.

I hope this information has been helpful to you.

Unit Two:
Mission Possible:
Always include the Required Basic Ingredients and Scholarship Non-Negotiables

Chapter III

Required Basic Ingredients #1:

Have the Right Attitude!

Required Basic Ingredients #1: Have the Right Attitude!

"Small decisions can profoundly impact your life." — Dr. J.P. Chisholm

What is more important than winning? In the world I live in and the situations that I encounter, I have learned that having a positive attitude can be more important than winning. Why is that? Well, I am glad that you asked. Because in my experience, there are times when you win, but don't gain. And in my specific case, I have learned more from losing, than I have ever learned from winning especially when I have the right attitude to receive and understand the life-lesson I am being taught in defeat.

Moreover, I believe that a positive attitude will help you more than your desire to win at everything. Because choosing to be positive in the midst of a storm, can help you to see the bigger picture. For example, having a positive attitude may help you realize that a storm represents a bad time and that bad times do not last forever. A positive attitude helps you see the bigger picture.

So, how do you define a winning attitude? I define a winning attitude as one that allows you see light even in a dark situation/place. Positivity can definitely do this for anyone. But it's a choice you have to consciously make so you are able to see the good and purpose in every situation. A winning attitude enables you to learn, and appreciate the lessons from losses.

It will also help you to overcome rejections, disappointments, and tough times.

How can this information be related to getting a scholarship?

Well, when you start applying for scholarships, awards, and other beneficial opportunities, if you are like most people, you will likely receive more rejections, than acceptances. When this happens, instead of allowing it to discourage you or make you quit, you will try to learn how the rejections can help you to improve your application.

Here are seven (7) steps to turn rejection into opportunity.

<u>Seven (7) Steps to Turning Scholarship Rejection into Opportunity</u>

So, you applied for a scholarship but did not receive it, instead you got a rejection.   Here are eight (8) steps to turn rejection into opportunity.

#1: Read the rejection letter to understand why you did not get the scholarship.

Read the rejection letter. Use it as a tool to understand why your application was rejected. This will help you to possibly address weaknesses in your application and improve on it.

Also, as a rule of thumb, after you have learned from it, don't dwell on it. Move forward in your purpose with the knowledge that the rejection just taught you how to become more impressive.

#2: Use the feedback given to you as constructive criticism.

Turn the feedback into an action step. As such, use the feedback as constructive criticism to make changes and updates to your other scholarship applications. This shows growth and a winning attitude.

#3: Contact the organization that rejected you and thank them for reviewing your scholarship application.

Make contact with the organization that rejected you and thank them with a "Thank You" Card or "Thank You" email. I will share some specific language for you to use in the next tip.

Please, note that you can do this with ease. Especially, since we know that the reviewing committee from your scholarship application is not your enemy. In fact, the scholarship committee may be super excited to review your application next time based on the positive character and winning attitude you have shown in sending them a thank you card in spite of your rejection.

#4: Inform the organization that you will use their constructive criticism to grow.

Prior to sending the scholarship committee or organization a thank you card, add a personal note to it saying you will use their constructive criticism to grow as a scholarship applicant. Additionally, notify the organization that you will use their feedback to try again at next year's scholarship opportunity.

#5: If you speak to a person, ask the person for their name and be super professional.

It's important to remember that first impressions count. As such, the impression that you make over the phone is just as important as the details included in your scholarship application. Because of this, it is important for you to remember to always be super nice and a true professional when interacting with the scholarship committee or any employee of their organization. Also, remember who you spoke to so you can ask for a specific person when following up for updates.

#6: Make follow-up calls and emails

After receiving the scholarship application, filling it out, and sending it back to the organization, follow-up with the organization via a phone call or email in two or three days. It is also a good idea to ask to speak with the person you met in #5. This is also the time to remember to be very polite, friendly, and super professional in your interactions as the person you are speaking with could in fact be in a position to choose you as the scholarship recipient. Also, as long as the particular scholarship rules allow, it is okay to ask the person if they can confirm receiving your scholarship application and if there are any other documents you need to send in.

7. Send a thank you letter to the committee

Once the scholarship committee has selected the scholarship recipient, whether you are selected or not, send the committee a thank you card for considering your application. This will convey to the committee that you are a mature person and may make you a standout applicant when you apply for the same scholarship next year.

Note: The thank you cards can easily be purchased from any dollar related store.

Hopefully, in following these seven (7) steps, you will improve your scholarship application and possibly have a greater chance at winning the scholarship, award, or other beneficial opportunity.

In following these steps, it will also allow you to put into action what it means to have the right attitude.

What if you don't receive the SAT/ACT score that you wanted?

If you took the SAT or ACT, but did not earn the score required to get accepted into the college of your choice. Instead of you seeing it as a rejection and thinking your future is over, ask yourself a simple question: What could I have done differently?

Possibly, this question will allow you to make a different decision such as 1) setting a study schedule; 2) signing-up for a tutoring service; 3) starting a consistent SAT/ACT practice program that provides feedback; or other strategy. As a byproduct of this, you take the test again and earn a higher score. This is putting the right attitude into action.

What if you are rejected by your college of choice?

Let's say, you apply to your college of choice and receive a letter of rejection, instead of you ripping it up and believing it is a sign the college is not in the cards for you, you contact the school directly and ask to speak to an admission's officer concerning "If there is anything else you can do to improve your application?" If they give you helpful feedback, act on the information accordingly. If not, use the rejection as a positive sign to give more energy and effort to your other college choices.

--

Here's the point. The right attitude can turn rejection into an opportunity that you can learn from, and use to work towards your goals.

I hope this chapter from my life has been helpful to you.

A Conversation With the Author:
Turning Rejection into Opportunity

One small decision I made that has greatly impacted my life was deciding to view "rejection" as an *opportunity* instead of as failure.

The shift in my perspective would open up the doors to one of the best experiences in my life.

It all happened rather quickly when I applied for admission to Florida State University in Tallahassee, Florida. I was rejected several times. A small decision to view rejection as an opportunity instead of as a failure motivated me to drive up to Tallahassee, Florida from Jacksonville, Florida (a 2-hour drive) after school one day and knock on the doors of the admission officers at Florida State University. There, I met with a lady who had worked so frequently with my file that she was familiar with me from my paperwork. When I mentioned my first name, she quickly recognized that I had been the person on her voicemail who had been respectfully asking for appeal after appeal of their admission decision. She said to me, "We [the Office of Admission] have made our decision on your behalf and you have *not* been accepted by Florida State." I responded by saying, "While that's what your letters said, I drove up here hoping you would meet again to make one final decision on my behalf." She reluctantly agreed only after making me promise that I would move on with my life regardless of their final decision.

After standing outside her door for about 15 minutes, the admission officer returned. In her hand was a small folded note. When I opened it, it had four simple words: "Welcome to Florida State!" My face lit up. I had been denied by several smaller colleges and yet, God had blessed me to be accepted into my number one university of choice. This small decision to drive to Tallahassee changed my life!

Despite how rough the admission road was, once I was enrolled as a student there, I was blessed to have won two major awards and received one mega distinction. The two major awards that I won were 1) *the Alpha Phi Alpha Fraternity, Incorporated College Brother of the Year Award* (for the State of Florida), and 2) I was the *FSU Homecoming King*. Lastly, I published my first book, *How to Make Your Past, a Blessing to Your Future*.

All of these were the result of one small decision that obviously had a big impact on my life. For me, the small decision was knocking on the admission officer's door that had told me "No!" The big impact was graduating from my number one college of choice, and the accomplishments that ensued.

Chapter IV

Required Basic Ingredients #2:
Make Time for What's Important and Stay Away from Negativity!

Required Basic Ingredients #2:
Make Time for What's Important and Stay Away from Negativity!

"Time is precious so make sure you spend it with the right people doing the right thing"
Dr. J.P. Chisholm

Can one small decision to change your circle of friends help you get a scholarship? It may sound like a simple question but answering the question is not as simple. Allow me to assist for just a moment with a follow-up question: Can a small decision ever get you into big trouble? Absolutely.

However, there are a lot of people that think that small decisions don't really matter...well, that is until they get you into trouble. In my experience, I have learned that the decisions we believe to be the smallest can sometimes have the greatest impact on who we are, what we do, what we represent, and what our future will look like. As such, one small decision can open up door after door of opportunities; while another small decision like not being mindful of who your friends are, and what they represent could get you arrested for life.

So, can one small decision to change your friend circle help you get a scholarship? It really depends on the type of friends you have. If your friends are positive people and working on their dreams just like you, then you have done an excellent job in selecting your friends because you and your friends can keep each other motivated.

However, if your friends are negative, toxic, and don't have any dreams, goals, or aspirations, then these friends of yours may not be the friends you want to keep around you especially when it's time to get down to business, work on your goals, and pursue scholarship opportunities.

One of the Basic Ingredients in our tools for success shared in *Mission Possible: How to Graduate From College Debt-Free* is to stay away or distance yourself from negative friends and negative people.

Why should you stay away from negative friends and negative people?

Here are five (5) reasons why you should stay away from negative (or toxic) friends and people while working on your scholarship goals:

1. Negative friends will not motivate you.

2. Negative friends may distract you from achieving your goals.

3. Negative friends may see going after scholarships as a waste of time because they are not willing to make the same positive decisions and choices that you are making. As such, they may try to influence you to waste your time instead of being productive.

4. Negative friends will not only pull you down, but they will pull you away in a different direction opposite of your goals.

5. Negative friends may drain your energy so there is nothing left in the tank to give towards a scholarship.

As one of the basic ingredients, *make time for what's important and stay away from negative friends*. This is a small decision that can have a great impact on your future. So, use your time wisely by sharing it with positive people that are on the same page as you. I hope this chapter has been helpful to you.

Chapter V

Required Basic Ingredients #3:
Use Your Creativity &
Incredible Ingenuity to
Overcome Walls

Required Basic Ingredients #3:
Use Your Creativity and Incredible Ingenuity to Overcome Walls

"As we grow older, we don't lose friends, we just learn who the real ones are."
Anonymous

What is the best way to get around a wall? Use <u>your</u> personal creativity and incredible ingenuity. My definition for **creativity** is *turning your imagination into something tangible that you can use to solve problems.* As for **ingenuity**, I see it *as being clever, resourceful, and inventive.* In my world, both creativity and ingenuity go hand-in-hand to create solutions to difficult problems. Also, by tapping into your personal creativity and incredible ingenuity, it can help you to earn scholarships.

<u>Creativity: How can I use my creativity to earn scholarships?</u>

In the context that I reference one's creativity, I am recommending that you use your talents, special abilities, and gifts to raise money for college. Moreover, in using your creativity as an important tool, you may amaze yourself with what you can accomplish.

For example, I have a list of creative ideas that you can use to raise money for college listed below. Please, note that some of these ideas will require special talents so if you have the gift or talent, use it for your creative edge, but if not, just try another idea on the list below.

Alternatively, here are ten (10) creative ideas that you can use to raise money for college.

Ten (10) Creative Ideas to Raise Money for College.

Here are ten (10) examples of creative ideas that you can use to earn money for college:

1. **Help edit student papers for money to go toward your college tuition.**

    In order to do this, you may need to reach out to former teachers in both high-school or middle school and inquire if they could share this information with their current students. Also, it may be helpful to post via social media and/or in the local library.

2. **Tutor other students in Math, Science, History, English or other subjects that you enjoy. enjoy**

Just as previously shared, in order to do this, you may need to reach out to former teachers in both high-school or middle school and inquire if they could share this information with their current students. Also, it may be helpful to reach out to local churches, community groups, after-school extended care programs for students, and the local library as well as make post about what you can do and who you can assist via social media. The children of family members and family friends may also become your future tutoring client.

3. **Play an instrument**

Contact your local church and inquire if you could participate in the band to be paid as a musician. Or, try to get paid to play your instrument at a local community event and inform the host or program sponsor that they can pay you by making a generous donation to your college fund.

4. **Display your art in a local art show**

Although it may take a bit of homework on your part to find a local art venue to share your work, there may be an art show that may offer a scholarship or cash prize to the winner. In any case, the award can be added to your college fund.

5. Design logos, websites, and other graphics

Although it may take a bit of homework on your part in connecting with the right audience, you may be able to solicit your services to friends, family members, former teachers, community leaders, coaches, and others. As such, once you connect with the right person that is interested in your services, share with them that you are able to design a logo, website, or other graphics for them and their business. The cost for your service could be a specific amount or a generous donation to your college fund.

6. Participate in a building or robotics competition with a cash prize

If you love building blocks or grew up playing with building blocks and building things, look for a local competition in your area. These competition will usually award participants with a Certificate for competing, which could be included on your college resume as an extra-curricular activity. Additionally, some of these competitions will award the winner with a scholarship and/or cash prize.

7. Baby sit for cash to be applied to your college fund

If you are a responsible person and don't mind spending time with young people that are in need of temporary supervision while their parents are away, share your time and baby-sitting - services with a family member as a dependable and reliable Baby-Sitter. Also, please, notify the person that hires you for these services that they will be saved and applied to your college fund, which may make the parents want to hire you more for professional services and to support an awesome cause—your future college education.

8. Dog sit or pet-sit for cash to be added to your college fund.

If you are a person that loves spending time around domestic animals like cats and dogs, then this will be a perfect opportunity for you to use your interest to earn money for college.

9. Repair a cell phone, personal computer (PC), or laptop

Can you fix a broken cell phone, laptop, or personal computer? If so, people will pay you handsomely to repair one of their favorite technological devices. Use what you earn to pay for college!

10. Use social media to stay connected and raise funds for college

Use your social media account (s) to connect or reconnect with former teachers, mentors, role-models, people who gave you a business card, friends of your parents/guardian, and others. Use this account to post about future college plans, current college plans and college updates. At the end of each post, be sure to add a one sentence liner like "Please, make a donation to my college fund!"

I hope you are able to use some of these ideas to raise money for college. However, before selecting the ideas you would like to try, please research what amount others have been able to charge from these services or similar ones in your local area. This will help you to set a competitive rate to earn from using your gifts, talents, and abilities.

Moreover, this is not an exhaustive list, but merely a handful of tangible ideas you can use as a creative means for earning money for college. Please, feel free to use these ideas at your discretion. Now, let's address ingenuity.

Ingenuity

In simple terms, a person that has ingenuity just knows how to be resourceful; they will find a way to make things work-out. Moreover, when it comes to *Mission Possible: How to Graduate Debt-Free*, ingenuity is important because a person that possesses ingenuity will see an opportunity that others may not.

Learn to use your ingenuity to step out and create opportunities that will help you to earn money for college. Below, I have six (6) examples of resourceful ideas that I believe you could use to raise money for college.

Six (6) Real Resourceful Ideas that you can use to Raise Money For College

Here are Six (6) ways that you can use resourcefulness to pay for college tuition.

#1: Create a *GofundMe* Page. Use social media to raise money for scholarships by making a post on your social media account and asking your friends and followers to make a donation to you via *GoFundMe* or a similar link.

#2: Get letters of recommendations from past and present teachers, guidance counselors, church leaders, employers, and other people that believe in you and how awesome you are as a person. Whenever you apply for a scholarship, include at least four (4) letters of recommendation. This resourceful strategy will be discussed in more detail in **Chapter VII**.

#3: Host a graduation party and charge an admission fee that you disclose will be used to cover your first year of college. Please, encourage people to give more.

#4: For every birthday, reach out to parents, family members, and friends and ask them to donate to your college fund.

#5: Volunteering is fun and can also earn you a scholarship. Inquire with the volunteer organization to learn if it awards scholarship opportunities to its volunteers. In the event that the organization does award scholarships to its volunteers, learn what steps you will need to take to apply as a volunteer.

#6: Have a job? Some jobs offer scholarship to their employees. Some of these scholarships are so generous they will even pay for a full semester to an employee. Do your homework to find the jobs that will offer scholarships to its employees. If the job has such an opportunity, inquire about the program, learn what you will need to do to apply, and apply for it.

For other specific examples of using creativity and ingenuity to raise money for school, please, feel free to jump around to various chapters. I also recommend you visit our website: www.GraduateDebtFreeClub.com to learn about what others did using creativity and ingenuity to raise money for college. Hopefully, you will apply a strategy that works best for you that we can share with others on our website.

I hope this chapter has been a blessing to you.

A Conversation With the Author:
Try Using Creativity and Ingenuity Instead of Credit Cards

Am I against using credit cards to pay for college? Yes I am! Unless, it is being used responsibly in an emergency situation and there is absolutely no other option. This view comes from the financially irresponsible way credit cards are being used to pay for college expenses without attempting to use any other options. What's even more difficult to explain is just how much credit card debt sets so many people back for so many years in the long-run.

Although one small decision, like applying to college or implementing one of the steps in this chapter can change your life for the best. Unfortunately, making one poor decision like running up credit card debt too soon and irresponsibly can also ruin it. So, think twice before using a credit card to pay for college unless you have a genuine, no other options emergency.

Instead, try using your creativity and ingenuity as often as you can to raise money for college. Your future will thank you for tapping into your personal creativity and resourcefulness. I pray this information has been a blessing to you.

Chapter VI

Required Basic Ingredients #4:
Focus on What's Best for YOU!

Required Basic Ingredients #4:
Focus on What's Best for You!

"Selfishness can be a good thing when you learn it is absolutely ok to advocate for yourself and on behalf of yourself." – Dr. J.P. Chisholm

Is it ever okay to be selfish? I along with so many other people have personally struggled with this question for many years. But, during my college years and beyond, I have learned an invaluable lesson on selfishness. The lesson learned is that it is not selfish to take care of yourself, but it's smart and healthy. Especially when it comes to focusing on your future, your mental health, your personal well-being, your integrity, or doing what's in your overall best interest. So if someone has called you selfish for doing what's best for you, I don't think you are the one with the problem because it's smart and healthy for you to do what's best for you.

By learning to do this at the right time, you have made yourself the priority and this is important for your overall positive mental health, well-being, and development. In doing this, you have made another small decision that could have a great impact on your overall success, life, and future.

So, how else can selfishness be a good thing? Here are five reasons that will explain how being selfish with your time could be both smart and healthy.

Five (5) Reasons to Explain how Being Selfish can Be Smart and Healthy

The following five (5) reasons expressed below will prove how being selfish is both smart and healthy for you.

1. To protect your mental health and stability

It is 100% okay to be selfish about protecting your mental health and stability. Why? Because your mental health or emotional stability is needed for you to be successful. There are times when life will just throw you off. In these moments to avoid making a bad decision or a decision that can pull you in the wrong direction, it's absolutely okay to take time-out to selfishly work on your mental health and emotional stability. So be selfish about this, and you will thank yourself for making the right decision.

2. To protect your time

It is 100% okay to be selfish to protect your time. Why? Because there comes a point in life when you realize that time is limited and you don't want to waste it by giving it away to people, places, and things that don't appreciate it. So, make it count by selfishly protecting your time from things that are trying to waste it.

3. To use your time wisely to pursue your goals

By being selfish with your time, you are protecting your time from fruitless pursuits and people that will waste your time away. Additionally, you can use those precious moments of time to pursue your personal goals and apply for scholarships, awards, and other beneficial opportunities. In doing so, you are using your time towards the big picture and to graduate from college debt-free.

4. You don't allow what others are saying to get in your head /or stop your progress.

As we have already established, being selfish can be both healthy and smart. This can help you get a scholarship by allowing you to disconnect from the negative words or opinions of others and focus on accomplishing your goal.

As such, please, note that worrying about the negative concerns or negative opinions of others can put your mind in a never-ending cycle that will only gradually drain you and stifle your progress. Because of this, don't waste your time or energy on what others are saying or allow it get in your head.

5. **It may reveal that you and your peers are moving in different directions.**

As you may have heard of the old adage, *"Birds of a feather,* flock together." What this means is that you and the people around you may have a great deal of things in common. Because of this, you may be able to influence your friends and they can influence you. By realizing that you and your peers are birds of a feather and on the same page, this may encourage you to buckle down and work together to accomplish goals and pursue your dreams.

However, you may also realize that you and your peers are not on the same page and because of this, you have not made much progress towards pursuing your personal goals as well as applying for scholarships, awards, and other benefits due to the negative influence of the people around you.

In this case, it may be wise to remember that it's okay for you to be selfish to work on achieving your goals. Additionally, spending less time with a negative or toxic person/group is both healthy and a mature display of positive decision-making.

So, if it is about making a decision that is in your best interest, it is okay to be selfish. This is a small decision with an incredible impact, and the reason it is considered one of the basic ingredients for *success*.

Moreover, as you prepare to apply for scholarships, if someone tries to make you feel bad about doing what's in your best interest, just remember you are making an excellent decision to do what's best for you. But also keep in mind that the decision you are making will have vast and far reaching implications as it relates to you finding money for college, going to college, protecting your emotional and mental health, personal well-being, and your overall success as a person.

So, unleash yourself and it will release your potential. Use this freedom to go after your dreams to raise money for college and ace your goal of graduating debt-free. I pray this chapter has been helpful to you.

Chapter VII

Scholarship
Non-Negotiables

Scholarship Non-Negotiable

"There is no shame in not knowing; the shame lies in not finding out." Russian Proverb.

What is a Scholarship Non-negotiable? Scholarship Non-Negotiables are the required task that you must do with each and every application that is <u>not</u> up for debate. These task are fundamentally important to elevate your application so that you are considered a top applicant for any scholarship, award, and/or beneficial opportunity. In this chapter, I will share the Mission Possible Top Five (5) Scholarship Non-Negotiables that you **are required** to include in every scholarship application to help you to get your scholarship application highly regarded.

The Mission Possible Top Five (5) Scholarship Non-Negotiables

Here are the top five (5) scholarship non-negotiables that you will need to include with every scholarship application.

1. **Include An Updated Resume – Please include this with every scholarship you apply for.**

Here is a sample for your review. Also, if you need a template for a resume, please visit our website:

www.GraduateDebtFreeClub.com and download a free template for you to use.

2. **Include Four (4) Letters or Recommendation – Please include these four (4) Letters of Recommendation with every scholarship application**

Contact people that will share just how amazing you are. Some people to consider for your letters of recommendation are your Teachers, Guidance Counselors, Pastors, Community Leaders, and other people that know you well. Please share with them the specific details concerning what the letter of recommendation will be used for (i.e., college acceptance or scholarship) and ask them to make the letter general enough so that it could be used again and again for multiple opportunities.

Also, always include four (4) letters of recommendation even if the scholarship committee is asking for less. At minimum, by giving four (4) letters of recommendation, it may help you to appear as a well-prepared and gifted applicant that is deserving to be considered as a top applicant.

3. **Include a Financial Letter with every scholarship application**

What is a financial letter? The financial letter is a personal statement from you expressing how important this scholarship is to you and your family. It will explain to the scholarship committee just how important you need this scholarship and how much it would mean to you.

4. Include a Personal Essay that High-lights you Turning Adversity Into Something Good.

Include a personal statement. Be sure to include an *adversity turn into something good-like story*. This is a story that highlights the adversities that you have faced and shares how have been able to overcome it. Alternatively, the story will share a moment of your life in which you turned adversity into an opportunity. I have included a few examples below for your reference.

Adversity Examples	Turning Adversity Into Something Good
Example #1: My family was homeless.	Example #1 Response: In spite of the homeless, I was able to maintain perfect attendance, take advanced classes, and graduate with an impressive GPA.
Example #2: No one in my family has attended college.	Example #2 Response: In spite of this fact, I have been able to earn a high GPA, SAT/ACT Scores, and pass my AP Exams while also mentoring

	elementary students on "Not Giving Up Their Dreams."
Example #3: I have a Low SAT / ACT Scores.	Example #3 Response: But I maintained a high GPA, served my community as a volunteer, and participated in scholastic and athletic extra-curricular activities. In these extra-curricular activities, I have serve as the President, VP, and Treasurer of my student organization as well as the Captain of the High-School Team that you participate on.

5. Send the Scholarship Committee a thank you card!

Remember to include a thank you card with every scholarship application that you send off.

Please, include the aforementioned four (4) scholarship non-negotiables and thank you card with every scholarship application that you apply for.

Also, once you receive your first scholarship, please, share your story with us on our website: www.GraduateDebtFreeClub.com. In sharing your story with us, we will highlight your scholarship journey and share your empowering story with others. I hope this information has been helpful to you.

A Conversation With the Author:
"I am who I am" Poem

Although not a basic ingredient, but one of the edges that I have used to earn scholarships, become a member of Youth Leadership Jacksonville's Class IX, receive a place in the Upward Bound Pageant, and earn a spot on FSU's Homecoming Court, which opened the doors to becoming FSU's Homecoming King during my undergrad years is the *"I am who I am" Poem*. This special poem is dear to me and I have often included it in my personal statements as well as during scholastic interviews to showcase my confidence and explain to the committee *who I am* and *who I am not*.

If you would like to add some pizzazz to the basic ingredients, spice it up by adding an "**I am who I am**" Poem to your scholarship application and/or interview (if offered). It is a great 14 -line poem to include because it allows you to showcase your confidence, talents, and tells your listeners how amazing you are. It is also in free verse so it doesn't have to rhyme. I included a template below to help you write your, "I am who I am" Poem.

"I am who I am"

Not Someone who _____.

Not Someone who _____.

Not Someone who _____.

Not Someone who _____.

And Not Someone who you or anyone else wants me to be.

But just who I am.

Someone who is _____.

Someone who is _____.

Someone who is _____.

Someone who is _____.

Someone who is me.

And this is who I am.

*Add your name: _____.

*Add an incredible fact about yourself_____.

Please, include your *"I am who I am"* Poem with every scholarship applications and share it with us on our website: **www.GraduateDebtFreeClub.com**.

I hope the "I am who I am" Poem will give you some additional ideas to sprinkle a little pizzazz to your scholarship applications. I hope this chapter has been a blessing to you.

Chapter VIII

Be Deliberate in Your Decision-Making!

Be Deliberate
In Your Decision-Making!

"I believe in the mantra that the more time you have, the more opportunities are available to you." —Dr. J.P. Chisholm

What does it mean to be deliberate in your decision making? Well, other than GPA, SAT/ACT, the basic ingredients and scholarship non-negotiables, being deliberate in your decision making is the final important quality that we will discuss in this chapter to help you to get a scholarship, award, or other beneficial opportunity. In being deliberate, it means you are *intentional* with your actions and *aware* of the decisions that you are making. In other words, the goal is to be present, not robotic. This is important in tailoring your scholarship application to the award instead of sending off a generic application. This small level of detail is a small decision that can help you to leave an indelible mark during your scholarship process.

Here are five deliberate decisions that will help you earn a scholarship.

Five (5) Deliberate Decisions that Will Help You to Earn a Scholarship

Below are five (5) deliberate decisions that will help you to earn a scholarship. Please, put a check inside the small box beside the item in order to document your accomplishment of completing it. Remember book rule #2, you can *write in me*!

❑ **1. Open an account for the sole purpose of saving money for college**

The small decision to open an account with the specific purpose of saving money for college could have a huge impact on helping you graduate from college debt-free. This account can be shared with family and friends for them to make donations towards your college aspirations and goal of graduating debt-free. This will also help you to save and track funds that have been received for this purpose.

Additionally, having a separate account for college expenses will help you distinguish what you have raised for college and what you have saved for other purposes. Please, research financial institutions that allows you to open a free bank account without hidden bank charges.

Once you have completed this step, please, check the box.

□   **2. Start applying for scholarships early**

I believe in the mantra that the more time you have, the more opportunities are available to you. As such, the more time you have, the more time you can use to apply for scholarships, awards, and other beneficial opportunities. So, don't wait to apply! Instead, start applying now.

By doing so, you may find scholarship opportunities that are only available to you right now because you have the time to look for them. As such, you may also be able to raise more funds towards your goal to graduate from college debt-free. So, use your time wisely and look for scholarship opportunities can apply for right now. Please, visit *Unit Three, Unit Four, and Unit Five* to learn more about specific scholarships, websites, and other opportunities to help you cover the cost for tuition, housing, and books.

Once you start searching for scholarships, awards, or other beneficial opportunities, please, check the corresponding box above. I am proud of you and the steps you are taking.

□   **3. Connect with others that can write you letters of recommendation**

Reach out to others that can write you letters of recommendation for admission into your college of choice and scholarship applications. I would highly recommend you to contact your current and former teachers, school guidance counselors, club advisors, coaches, church leaders, organizational sponsors, employers, volunteer coordinators, mentors, and others that will share amazing things about who you are as a person and the positive character you possess.

Please, try to get at least four (4) letters of recommendation that are general enough for you to use to apply for multiple scholarships, awards, and other beneficial opportunities.

Once you have your four (4) letters of recommendation, please, check off the corresponding box above.

❑ **4. Be nice to everybody!**

Be kind to everyone. This is a small decision that can have a huge impact because you never know who people really are, who they know, and what they can do to either assist you to reach your goals or stifle your progress. Because of this, I personally believe that if you are kind to others and treat others with respect (in spite of how they treat you), I believe that kindness will return back to you based on the premise that *you reap what you sow*.

So, what does *"you reap what you sow"* mean? It means that when you are kind, nice, and pleasant to others, those same positives that you put out will come back to you. Possibly, it will come back to you in the form of a stellar letter of recommendation or a school official or community leader telling you about an exclusive scholarship opportunity because you are a nice person or have an amazing reputation. Or, someone vouching for you at just the right time. So, as a rule of thumb, be nice and pleasant to others and it may come back to you.

Once you begin making deliberate efforts to be kind, nice, and pleasant to others, please, check off the corresponding box above.

❑   **5. Respect the process of applying for scholarships like you would a job.**

One final small decision that can have a huge impact is for you to treat application for scholarships, awards, and other beneficial opportunities the way you would treat a job. What does that mean, set a few hours aside from week to week and treat those hours set aside as *"work hours."* But, instead of going to work during this window, you will use it exclusively to apply for scholarships, awards, and other beneficial opportunities.

As a personal recommendation, I would recommend you to put at least fifteen (15) to twenty (20) hours aside from week to week. During this window, treat your time as uninterrupted "work hours" that you are using to do your job of applying for scholarships, awards, and other beneficial opportunities. During this same time window, give it the respect you would give a serious job opportunity by not talking on the phone or texting friends during this window of time; getting distracted by television, the internet, or social media during this window of time; or doing something else that takes your concentration away from the job.

Once you take deliberate steps to set time aside to apply for scholarships, awards, and other beneficial opportunities the way you would treat a job, please, check off the corresponding box above.

--

If you have been successful in achieving these five (5) deliberate and impactful decisions, I congratulate you! Well done! ! However, if you have not been able to check off all of these initial small steps, then I encourage you to continue to strive to do so and work towards the objective of checking off all five (5). Moreover, by accomplishing these initial, small, and deliberate decisions, they will help you to achieve your goals of graduating debt-free.

I pray this insight from me has been helpful to you.

Unit Three:
Mission Possible: Finding Money for College Tuition

Chapter IX

Finding and Applying for College Scholarships

Finding and Applying for College Scholarships

"Getting a scholarship has nothing to do with luck but the work you are willing to put into the process" —Dr. J.P. Chisholm

Is earning all A's or making the AB Honor-roll the only way to earn a scholarship? Absolutely not.

Having good grades is an awesome accomplishment and very commendable! It proves that you went to school, worked hard, and did the things you were supposed to do in school.

However, scholarships are not just available for students with stellar grades. There are a plethora of scholarships available for all types of students and for a bevy of different reasons. The focus of this chapter will help **all** students earn scholarships regardless of the grades you made in school.

In this chapter, the only prerequisite that you will need to adhere to is the following:

1) Give yourself plenty of time;
2) Be diligent and deliberate in your pursuit to find money for college;
3) With every scholarship application, award, or other beneficial opportunity, include the

Mission Possible Basic Ingredients (*See Chapter 3 to Chapter 8*); and
4) Apply for every scholarship that is in line with your strengths

Now, let's go find some free money to cover the cost of college tuition.   Remember to include the basic ingredients and a thank you card with every scholarship application. For more information about the basic ingredients, please, revisit Chapter 3 to Chapter 8.

How can I find scholarship money for tuition?

In order to find scholarship money to cover the cost of college tuition, you should <u>first</u> learn more about the categories for scholarships that cover tuition and organize your scholarship pursuit based on the category that would be the easiest for you to get a scholarship. The Three (3) categories are shared below:

o **National Scholarships**
o **State Specific Scholarships**
o **Local Scholarships**

What are the Three (3) Scholarship Categories in Mission Possible for College Tuition?

The Three (3) Scholarship Categories for College Tuition that we will focus on in this chapter are **state scholarships, national scholarships, and local scholarships.** Let's discuss each one starting with **state scholarships**.

What type of student/scholarship applicant should first apply for a state specific scholarships?

If you are a student/applicant looking for scholarships that recognize and award students that have earned exceptional grades, high honors and achievements, and have impressive test scores, start your scholarship pursuit with state scholarships.

State scholarships may be offered to a limited group of students by a high-school guidance officer, college admissions officer, state scholarship representative, or similar person based on the graduating student's GPA, SAT/ACT Test-scores, class-rank, academic rigor, and other similar factors. Some state scholarships are limited to students that have graduated within the top 10% to top 20% of their respective student body or graduating class. As such, students with an exemplary GPA and test-scores may find it easier to qualify for state scholarships.

So, apply for scholarships that you would be a strong candidate. If you have an exemplary GPA and impressive test scores, start your scholarship search for state scholarships. Other scholarship applicants that may best qualify for state scholarships include the following types of student:

- a graduating student that has an excellent GPA or SAT/ACT test score;
- a student that is considered a high-achiever in the top of his/her graduating class;
- a student that has high honors and achievements that would become a first generation college student.

If any of this sounds like you, then you should make applying for state scholarships your first priority.

How can I Find a State Scholarship?

State scholarships can often be found by simply talking to your high-school guidance counselor, school scholarship officer, college admissions officer, state scholarship representative, or similar person. Occasionally, the person may email you a link to a state website and may share some information to help you apply. Please, also note that some state scholarships may be in the form of scholarships and post-secondary grants.

Alternatively, some state specific scholarships and state grants can also be learned about using the internet and taking the following steps:

- o **Step #1: Go to *Google.com*.**
- o **Step #2: Use *Google* to search the internet using the phrase: *www.Financialaidfinder.com* and <u>*your*</u> *specific state*.**

If done correctly, several scholarships in your specific state should appear in your search.

Alternatively, other state specific scholarships can also be learned about using the internet and taking the following steps below:

- **Step #1: Go to *Google.com*.**
- **Step #2: Use *Google* to search using phrase *"scholarship.com"* and *your specific state*.**

If done correctly, using Google search phrase, "scholarship.com" and your specific state, a list of scholarships in your state should appear.

For more information on state scholarships, please visit our website: www.GraduateDebtFreeClub.com.

Hopefully, these strategies will lead you to several state scholarships. Let's address the next scholarship category, which are **local scholarships.**

What type of student should apply first for a local scholarship?

If you are a student looking for scholarships that will recognize and award a student for being super involved in school-related activities or serving as a mentor and role-model for younger students through an after-school program, and other community-service related projects in your local community, start your scholarship search looking for local scholarships. This type of student does well when applying for local scholarships as he/she may often be considered a "home town hero," which is a very special and beloved credential for a student.

Based on what the student has done for his/her local community, others may also regard the student as a "home town hero" because this student is known within the community as someone that will go to college, do an excellent job while in college, return home to the local community, and be a credit to the community.

Interestingly, based on what the student has accomplished for the community and through the community, having the best GPA and SAT/ACT may not be the most important consideration for the student applying for a local scholarship. Instead, students that are involved in their local community, render community service, and participate in a myriad of extracurricular activities with a good GPA may find it easier to qualify for local scholarships.

Moreover, apply to scholarships that you would be a strong candidate for. If you are involved in your local community, have plenty of recorded hours of community service, and are involved in several extracurricular clubs and organizations, start your scholarship search with local scholarships.

Other scholarship applicants that may best qualify for local scholarships include the following types of student:

o   Local scholarships aimed at certain communities, neighborhoods, schools, and other demographics;
o   Local scholarships aimed at spouses of certain groups or children of certain groups;
o   Local scholarships aimed at members of a local organization, association, club, or church in the community.

How can I Find Local Scholarships?

Here are seven (7) important tips that will help you to find local scholarships and earn scholarships from them.

1. Contact civic clubs, organizations, associations, fraternities, sororities, churches, non-profits, and other similar groups in your local area.

Start your scholarship search for local scholarships by contacting civic clubs, organizations, associations, fraternities, sororities, churches, and other similar groups in your local area. The specific information to contact these various groups in your specific area can be easily found by using one of the following ways:

- Search the internet for the name, address, and website of the aforementioned specific groups in your area.
- Visit YellowPages.com
- Use a city's online phone book or printed phone book

Next, search for or find the section on *civic clubs, organizations, associations, fraternities, sororities, churches, non-profits, and other similar-related groups in your local area.* Contact each of the listed groups and inquire if it offers a scholarship that you can apply for.

Please, note that the person you speak to may be able to give you the details on how to pick up the scholarship (i.e., mail it, email it, or personal pick-up) as well as how to apply for it and its deadline.

Also, please, note that it is important to be kind, nice, and pleasant as possible as the person that picked up the phone or the person that may have shared the scholarship details with you may in fact be on the scholarship committee. So, make a good first impression because little things like making a positive first impression could play a significant role in determining who gets the scholarship. This is also a great example of how small decisions could have a material impact. See chapter X to learn more on this topic.

Lastly, even if you <u>do not</u> receive the scholarship or it has already been awarded, be sure to mail the organization a thank you card so that they can remember you next time.

2. Apply for the scholarships that are closest to your home first.

Because I have known local scholarship committees to favor local hometown heroes and amazing student accomplishments in the area that a person resides, in order to earn a scholarship, I recommend applying for scholarships closer to home before applying to others.

Also, in applying for local scholarships closest to your home (or area that you live in) first and working your way out, you may learn that some local scholarships in your community may give scholarship priority to local students that live, work, and go to school in the area. So, apply for the scholarships in your community first and then get your application out to other areas and communities.

3. Ask Others for Advice

If you have friends, family members, or know of others that may have received the same local scholarship in a previous year, <u>and only if</u> it is not a violation of the scholarship rules, try to get some insight from the person that has already received the award. It may be helpful to simply ask the person that you know the following two (2) questions:

o **What information did you include in your scholarship application?**

o **And is there anything they did that may have made their scholarship application stand out?**

Please, note that if the person shares something of substance, use their insight with your local scholarship application. For example, if the person shares that they received it because the committee was impressed with their community service projects, then submit your application with all of the **scholarship basics, non-negotiables,** and add information concerning community service projects that you have also completed, thereby improving your application.

4. Tell the Truth; Honesty and Reputation Matters

Also, when applying for a scholarship, always tell the truth! Your ability to be honest and the reputation that you have established matters. Don't take shortcuts by engaging in deceptive practices, sharing false information, and by not being 100% truthful. Telling the truth matters! Your reputation matters! Don't tarnish what you have worked so hard to establish by engaging in dishonesty.

5. Visit your local school and look for student organization or other groups that award scholarship funds.

Find out the criteria to apply for the award. Let the club advisor or club sponsor know that you are interested in the award. Apply for it! You never know, these organizations may open up the doors to you receiving a scholarship.

6. Try to find out about local scholarships for volunteers in your area.

Look for voluntary scholarship awards. You may be able to find out about these from your local school guidance counselors, volunteer coordinators, or other community group leaders that are involved with your school.

Alternatively, you may be able to learn more about volunteering scholarships through your local community service organizations, service groups in your area, and community service initiatives through your local college or university.

7. Apply for scholarships at conferences.

Find out about conferences and other similar activities in your area and if they have a local scholarship. Find out how to apply for the conference scholarship and apply for it. Interestingly, you may be amazed to learn that several students attend student conferences, but do not apply for these types of scholarships. This information may work in your favor if you attend the conference, learn about the scholarship, and apply for it.

For more information on local scholarships, please, visit our website: www.GraduateDebtFreeClub.com.

Hopefully, these strategies will lead you to several local scholarships. Now, let's address the next scholarship category, which are **national scholarships.**

What type of student should apply for a national scholarship?

If you are a well-rounded student with a lot of accomplishments (evidenced by a solid resume) in various areas such as leadership positions, academic accomplishments, community service projects, maintain a positive self-esteem, and you don't mind writing an occasional essay to receive a scholarship, you should start your scholarship search looking for national scholarships.

Additionally, student government leaders, class-officers, and students that have participated in internship programs with solid GPA and test-scores may also be great matches for national scholarships as these scholarships tend to look for the overall well-rounded student applicant.

How can I Find National Scholarships?

National scholarships can usually be found via online scholarship searches and databases using one of the following websites below:

- ❑ *www.Fastweb.com*
- ❑ *www.Scholarships.com*
- ❑ *www.BrokeScholar.com*

- *www.Cappex.com*
- *www.Financialaidfinder.com*

These websites are usually easy to use and open to any potential applicant interested in applying for the scholarship (even if the applicant does not meet the scholarship specifications).

Is there any way to ensure that I will receive a scholarship?

No, there is not a way to guarantee that you will receive a scholarship. However, there are several things you can do to increase your chances of receiving one. Here are five (5) possible ways to increase your chances of receiving a scholarship.

Five (5) Possible Ways of Increasing Your Chances of Receiving a Scholarship

1. Start applying early; give yourself plenty of time

Start applying as early as possible. In some cases, this may mean starting your application process towards the end of your junior year (**11th grade**) in high school. Alternatively, it could be laying out a scholarship plan as to what you will apply for. *See Unit One and the Mission Possible: "I am*

Possible" notebook for additional support in making your Mission Possible Scholarship Plan of Action.

2. Always include a resume that celebrates who you are and what you have accomplished.

With every scholarship application, always include a resume with a cover letter that celebrates who you are and what you have accomplished. Also, make sure your resume is tailored to the specific scholarship award. Don't hold back in fear that it will make you look overqualified; use your resume to celebrate you by sharing all of the things you have accomplished.

For example, be sure to include things like: subjects that you tutor, languages that you can speak, skills, places that you have traveled/lived outside the US, jobs, internships, volunteer hours, experiences, and leadership positions held in school, church, community, and other involvements.

Also, revisit chapter 3 to chapter 8 for all the **Mission Possible** *Required Basic Ingredients and Scholarship Non-Negotiables to include.*

3. Add at least four (4) Letters of Recommendation

Try to include at least four (4) letters of recommendation even it's more letters than required by the scholarship. For example, if the scholarship does not ask for letters of recommendation, as a default, include four (4) letters of recommendation.

However, if the scholarship does ask for at least two (2) letters of recommendation, go ahead and include an additional two (2). The exception to not including more is if the application explicitly limits you by requesting that you do not include any additional letters of recommendation.

4.   Make sure your application is neat and well organized.

It is a joy for a person reviewing a scholarship applications to look over a neat application. However, when your application is neither neat or well organized, your accomplishments can easily be overlooked and your application may not be taken seriously.

For example, make sure you print your resume on resume paper (32 lbs. premium weight linen paper with 100% cotton or similar paper sold at office supply stores); make sure you type or print out your application instead of handwriting it; that the paper you use is not creased, smelly, or has spill stains, or other unnecessary markings; that there were no streaks in the printing due to your ink cartridge needing to be refilled or replaced. By making sure that these elements are addressed, your application will look very neat and well organized.

5.   Go for scholarships that also require an essay.

Apply for scholarships that also require an essay. Fortunately for you, this may increase your chances of applying as other capable candidates may not have applied for this particular scholarship solely because the person did not want to write an essay. As a rule of thumb, do the things that others won't. Use your time wisely to craft an essay as required by the scholarship and apply for it.

Which scholarship category should you pursue first?

After asking yourself which scholarship category to pursue first, the answer is likely the category that will be the easiest for you to get.

If you have difficulty choosing which category to pursue first, I have shared a chart below to help you choose which scholarships to pursue first based on your strengths. In the chart, I am merely sharing commentary that I believe is helpful, but you are not required to follow it.

Please, note that if you see the word *"1st"* under one category based on a certain skill or strength, it is suggesting that you pursue this category first to start your scholarship pursuit. Alternatively, if you see the word, "1st" in two or more categories at the same time, it means that you can choose either category to start your scholarship pursuit.

Lastly, it is highly recommended that you set time aside to apply for scholarships in every category. Please, see the chart below as a suggestive tool I created to help you get started with the type of scholarship you should apply to 1st based on your specific strengths. I hope you find it helpful. See chart details below.

Your Strengths	National Scholarships	State Scholarships	Local Scholarships
High GPA		1st	
Impressive SAT/ACT		1st	
Local Student Hero			1st
Celebrated on Local News			1st
Have Time to Apply Early	1st		
Has Traveled Aboard	1st		
Super Involved with extracurricular activities	1st		1st
SGA Pres	1st		1st
Senior Class Pres	1st		1st
Class Pres.	1st		1st
Student Leader	1st		1st
Top 10%		1st	
Top 20%		1st	
High GPA + Community Service		1st	1st

+75 Recorded Community Service Hours	1st		1st
IB, AP, or Honors Student		1st	
Student Athlete	1st		1st
Welcomes Essay Writing	1st	1st	1st
Has an Internship	1st		

In applying for **any** of these scholarships, be sure to include the **Mission Possible Scholarship Non-Negotiables** listed below:

- Include an updated resume: Please, include this in every scholarship you apply for.

- Include four (4) letters or recommendation: Please, include these four (4) letters of recommendation in every scholarship application.

- Include a financial letter with every scholarship application.

- Include a personal essay that highlights you turning adversity in to something good.

For more information on the scholarship non-negotiables, please, reference **chapter 7**. Also, feel free to visit: www.GraduateDebtFreeClub.com to learn more.

I hope this extensive chapter from me has been a blessing to you.

A Conversation With the Author:
No School Loans. No School Debts.

Both my wife and I have never received any loans for school. In high school, she used the extra time she had during the course of her senior year to apply for several college scholarships (local, state, and national). She received several of the scholarships that she had applied for from churches, community groups, civic organizations, and from Florida State University. She used her scholarship money to pay for college and continued to apply for new scholarships as a student. Then, as a college student, she received a foreign language scholarship, which allowed her to study abroad for free in Spain and Italy for a summer. She also received room and board from a scholarship that gave her free housing and meals for the remainder of college. She worked on campus and used her gifts as a musician to earn additional income to pay for school. As a result, she graduated from college debt free.

In law school, she became an entrepreneur when she stepped out using one of her X-factors to start a college apparel retail store (www.famutshirts.com). She also bought a house that she used as a rental property, and still used her additional time and status as a student to earn academic scholarships to graduate debt free (without credit cards, student loans, etc.).

My story is similar. In high school, I applied for several local and national scholarships and received a number of them. I also received several leadership and community service awards. In addition, I worked at my college dorm as a resident assistant in exchange for free housing and meals. At the same time, I also worked for a research center and budgeted the money I earned to pay for school. Although it took some sacrifice and smart financial planning, I graduated debt free.

After graduating from college, I wanted to continue my education debt free. I decided to use my book sales of the second edition of *"How to Make Your Past a Blessing to Your Future"* (*ISBN: 978-0-9755110-0-8)* to pay for a program in Strategic Finance in Smaller Businesses that I completed at the Harvard Business School in Boston.

With the favor of God, and implementing the financial strategies included within my second book, *"Investitude"* (*ISBN: 978-0-9755110-1-5*), my wife and I both graduated debt-free and you can do the same.

I pray this chapter of my life blesses yours. I am also hopeful that you will share your debt free story with us and our online community. Please, visit *www.GraduateDebtFreeClub.com* to learn more.

Chapter X

Send Tuition Sponsorship Letters & Emails to Family Members & Friends

Send Tuition Sponsorship Letters and Emails to Family Members and Friends

"Don't let what you can't do interfere with what you can do."

Anonymous

Will friends and family members give you money for school? Sometimes I think it is easy for people to forget some of our greatest supporters are our friends and family members. In many cases, friends and family members are people who know who you are, what your character represents, and what you will do. Because of this, this group represents a strong support base that may be able to give you *something* towards your college tuition. And even though this group may not cover everything, it may give you just what you need to get started on your way to pay a portion of your college expenses in order to help you graduate debt-free.

How can I encourage friends and family members to give towards my college tuition?

Here are three (3) practical tips you can use to motivate your friends and family members to help you pay for college.

1. **Send a formal letter to friends or family members asking them to make a donation or contribution towards your cost for college.**

   I included a sample letter for your reference at *www.GraduateDebtFreeClub.com*. If you would like to use this letter as a template, please, visit our website to learn more as to how you can use it.

2. **Start a GoFundMe Page.**

   Start a GoFundMe Page designed to help you fund college tuition by sharing it with friends, family members, and others in your circle.

3. **Birthday Gift – Make a Deposit in my Scholarship Fund as a Birthday Gift!**

   On your birthday, ask your friends and families to make a financial gift or donation to your college, scholarship, or tuition fund as the ultimate birthday gift.

Why would family members and friends want to give to you in the first place?

I believe there are tons of reasons why friends and family members may support your initiative. One, they are your friends and family members. That means this is likely a group of people who would like to see you do well. Also, it's funny to admit it, but it's a lot harder to say no to close friends and family.

Also, friends and family members sometimes know more about us, than we know. As such, because they already know about the terrible past experience, the difficult upbringing, or the unexpected tragedy, even though they have never spoken to you about it, your friends and family members may admire your strength and may be looking for an opportunity to give to you as a way to show support and love. You informing them of what you need may allow them to show support through your college fund, scholarship fund, and/or college tuition.

I hope this chapter from me has been helpful to you.

A Conversation With the Author
You Get Back What You Give Out

When thinking of raising money by reaching out to friends and family members, some people will give to you because of the way you treated them. It's amazing how little some people think of others until they have a need. For me, I have always tried to plant positive seeds with others. It doesn't mean I did everything right, but I have always tried my best to treat others with respect.

Interestingly, when I reached out to others during my times of need, there were people who reached out to me that I didn't even know I had positively impacted. One was a friend of mine from freshman year at FSU. We both shared similar beliefs and would talk on occasion about a book that he was trying to encourage others to read about a carpenter.

As I was raising money to attend the program at Harvard and sent out letters to my friends and family members, he quickly responded by saying, **how much do you need?** I shared with him that I had a remaining balance of about $500.00. In my moment of need, he sent the remaining balance as an in-kind donation and I was blessed to attend the program.

Thank you, **Marcus Johnson** in Tampa, Florida for being an important part of my Graduate Debt-Free story.

I hope this chapter from my life has been a blessing to you.

Chapter XI

Tuition Reimbursement

Tuition Reimbursement

"Success lies not in being the best, but in doing your best." Anonymous

When looking for a job, what may be better than an hourly wage? Tuition reimbursement as a job benefit! Although, it may not be considered a scholarship, a tuition reimbursement program is a material job benefit that should be considered as a very real way to help you pay for college tuition and graduate debt-free. So, when thinking about college and having a job, don't just get a job for a pay-check; try to find a job with tuition reimbursement.

What is Tuition Reimbursement?

Tuition Reimbursement is a benefit offered by certain companies in which a portion of your education is paid for by your employer. Some companies offer this to both part-time and full-time employees as a way of attracting and maintaining the best employees.

If offered, tuition reimbursement programs vary based on company policy. So, if you already have a job, contact the Human Resources Department and inquire about tuition reimbursement and how to qualify for it.

However, if you are in need of a job and would like to use Tuition Reimbursement, research the companies in your area to learn if the companies offer tuition reimbursement and how it works. This information may help you narrow down your job prospects to only consider applying and working for a company with tuition reimbursement.

I hope this information has been helpful to you. For more information about companies that offer tuition reimbursement, please, visit us online at www.GraduateDebtFreeClub.com.

Chapter XII

Turning Contacts Into Partners In Education

Turning Contacts Into Partners in Education

"It takes a whole village to raise a child."
African Proverb

How many times do you meet people, get their contact info, but do not keep in touch? Plenty of people are met this way each and every day. Maybe we don't keep in touch because we do not have a reason to keep in touch outside of the random meetings or business networks this person shares with you. But the network between you and this person and what could be gained from the relationship could become invaluable to you by asking this person to become one of your *Mission Possible Partner's in Education*.

What is a Mission Possible Partner in Education?

A *Mission Possible Partner in Education* is a person that has agreed to partner with you to support your educational pursuits by being a mentor to you and to help you stay accountable. This is a person that will do the following:

1. Offer you mentorship and advice (if needed).
2. Receive monthly updates on your time in college via email updates

3. Make a generous donation to you once a year to help you pay for college.

How do I meet potential Mission Possible Partners in Education?

There are plenty of potential Mission Possible Partners in Education to meet. Please, note that a place to find potential *Mission Possible Partners in Education* could include the following:

o Conferences,
o Community events,
o Organizational events,
o Church functions,
o Business meetings (open to the public),
o Virtual club houses,
o Social media platforms, and
o Other places that allow people to socialize, network, and interact with each other.

How do I make someone a Mission Possible Partner in my Education?

1. You ask the person to be your Mission Possible Partner in Education.

After explaining the concept to the person, both high-school and college students can easily gain the support of others by asking them to become one of their mentors and *Mission Possible Partners in*

Education. You would likely need to explain to the person that as your mentor and *Mission Possible Partner in Education,* you would be relying on the person for mentorship, wise advice, letters of recommendation, and to make a once a year donation to your college tuition or scholarship fund (at whatever amount the person is comfortable doing).

2. Create an Online Newsletter Sent out by Email

Create an online newsletter for your Mission Possible Partners in Education. Allow the newsletter to share updates on you, what you are accomplishing, and learning in college.

Here are four (4) of the websites that you can use to create this free online newsletter below:

- *www.MailChimp.com*
- *www.Activecampaign.com*
- *www.FreeMailTemplates.com*
- *www.Cakemail.com*

3. Send out monthly updates to your Mission Possible Partner's in Education

Each month, send each of your *Mission Possible Partners in Education* a monthly update using one of the free newsletters that you create on your own. In the monthly newsletter include your monthly accomplishments as well as the courses you are taking each semester and the grades you have earned from each course. It may also make your Mission Possible Partners in Education feel special if you include a couple of pictures or videos in each newsletter.

4. Add new people that you meet to the newsletter

Also, every time you meet someone new that could potentially become one of Your Partners in Education, it may be a good idea to add them to your newsletter if you plan to ask the person to become one of your Mission Possible Partners in Education in the future.

5. Publically thank your Partners in Education and give them a *Mission Possible Partners in Education Certificate of Appreciation*

Once a year, invite your Partners in Education to a dinner (or meal covered by you) as a group or individually. At this gathering, recap on all of your accomplishments from each month or each semester as these accomplishments are also the ones you shared in your monthly newsletter.

Next, publically, thank all of your *Mission Possible Partners in Education* by name and be sure to tell them about the specific positive impact they have on your life.

Additionally, as an extra tribute to them and their support, feel free to present them with a *Mission Possible Partners in Education Certificate of Appreciation*, which can be freely downloaded and customized by you from our website: www.GraduateDebtFreeClub.com.

6. Ask Each of Your Mission Possible Partners in Education to continue being one for the next school year.

After you have celebrated your Mission Possible Partner's in Education, reach out to each of them and ask them if they will continue to be one of your *Mission Possible Partner's in Education* for an additionally year. Please, explain that this would mean that do the following:

- Offer you mentorship and advice (if needed)
- Receive monthly updates on your time in college
- Make a generous donation to you once a year to help you pay for college.

So, next time you are at a networking event or conference and you meet successful people, ask the person to become one of your **Mission Possible Partners in Education**. This team will keep you accountable while also helping you accomplish your goals.

I hope this chapter from me has been a blessing to you.

A Conversation With the Author:
Genuine Relationships with Others Matter

For you to be successful with your *Mission Possible Partners in Education*, try your best to have a genuine and true relationship with each of the Partners. This may also help each of the *Mission Possible Partners in Education* to feel genuinely appreciated while also allowing you to grow and learn from a successful person that you respect. Because of this, I encourage you to be honest with them, eager to learn from their experiences, and to ask questions concerning areas of their expertise. In doing so, overtime, you may gain more than just a *Mission Possible Partner in Education*, but a life-long supporter, mentor, and advocate.

I hope this chapter from me has been a blessing to you.

Chapter XIII

Prepaid College Programs: Planning for a College Education

Prepaid College Programs: Planning for a College Education

"The cards you hold in the game of life mean very little--it's the way you play them that counts."

Anonymous

What are we using to pay for the future education of our children? Florida Prepaid. Why? Because it is an easy, cost efficient, and reliable program to help pay for college. Also, in the future, if plans change, Florida prepaid will allow us to transfer the funds to possibly a sibling or close the plan and withdraw the remaining balance. Lastly, we are able to pay towards it gradually over the course of our children's adolescence into their teenage years instead of paying an unmanageable lump sum amount.

In this chapter, I will discuss Prepaid College Plans as a long-term solution for parents, legal guardians, and others serving in a similar capacity to help fund the college cost for your children. It is an effective way to gradually pay for the college aspirations of your children. Additionally, several of these accounts allow both friends and family members to make contributions to these accounts.

What is a Prepaid College Plan?

Many states in America offer prepaid college plans for students that are interested in going to college in a particular state. Many of the prepaid college programs will also lock in the current rates for students at the time the program is started (even if your child plans to go to college ten or fifteen years later). It is also helpful to note that in some of these prepaid college programs, parents are allowed to transfer the funds to other eligible children or withdraw funds if plans change.

What are the Benefits?

Although benefits vary by state, some of the common ones include:

- You can lock in tuition rates in the specific state of the prepaid college program.

- Your child's college tuition is gradually paid for throughout their childhood (which means the lump sum burden of paying for college doesn't fall on you on their high school graduation day).

- If your child receives scholarships or doesn't go to school in that particular state, some of the programs may allow you to transfer, withdraw, or refund the funds (which may include a minimal fee).

Please, consult your state's prepaid college program to learn more.

Are Prepaid College Programs Offered in Every State?

No, prepaid college plans are not offered in every state. Please, research your state to determine if a prepaid college plan is offered in your state.

If my state does not have a prepaid college program, what are my other options?

If a prepaid college plan is not offered in your state, try looking into a *529 College Saving Plan*. Although, these plans can vary by state, they are generally similar to Prepaid College Program since they allow you to save for college early on. Please, research *529 College Saving Plans* offered in your area to learn more.

How can I learn more about Prepaid College Programs and/or 529 College Saving Programs?

For starters, you can try visiting our website to learn more at www.GraduateDebtFreeClub.com.

A Conversation With the Author:
Other Uses for Prepaid College Money: Graduate School and Vocational Education

Did you know some states will allow you to use prepaid college money to also pay for vocational school and graduate degrees (Masters and Doctoral Degrees)? This is awesome news for any person interested in having the option to use prepaid money to cover the cost of a technical education, a career path related education, or going beyond an undergraduate degree to pursuing a Masters or Doctoral Degree. If these options are offered through a prepaid college program in your state, use it to your advantage explore your interest and to learn more about all of the educational paths available to you.

I hope this information from me has been helpful to you.

Unit Four:
Mission Possible: Covering the Cost of College Housing

Chapter XIV

Become a Resident Assistant (RA) or Community Assistant (CA)

Become a Resident Assistant (RA) or a Community Assistant (CA)

"An obstacle is something you see when you take your eyes off the goals you are trying to reach."

Anonymous

Did you know some students are allowed to work in the dorm in exchange for free room and board? One of the best opportunities I had as a college student was when I became a Resident Assistant (RA) (also referred to as a Community Assistant (CA)) at my college dormitory. This can be an excellent housing opportunity found both on campus and off campus at both school dorms and private dorms. In accepting this role of responsibility, the RA or CA is given free room and board and a meal plan. In this chapter, we will discuss some of the initial ways to help you to learn more about becoming an RA / CA in exchange for free room and board and a meal plan as well as what the role entails.

What is a RA or CA?

Well, in my opinion, being an RA or a CA is the coolest job on the planet for a college student. "RA" is for Resident Assistant. Alternatively, "CA" is for Community Assistant. Although the titles sound different, they both are the same job and may be used interchangeably.

Moving forward, being an RA/CA does require a bit of work on your part as you basically work in the dorm. Some of the work-related task include occasionally creating events and activities on your floor for the other student residents, making sure that other residents are always safe and following the rules, and you may have to do some front desk responsibilities like answering the phone and sitting at the front desk. But, in exchange for *free room and board* and *a meal plan* (as this may be offered at certain college resident halls and dormitories), being an RA/CA is a pretty sweet deal. Especially, if you continue as an RA/CA until you graduate from college.

Why become a Resident Assistant (RA) or Community Assistant (CA) at the Dorm?

Because being an RA/CA comes with free room and board. This means 100% of your housing cost is covered. If your college or dorm offers 100% free housing and a meal plan, you have a great opportunity to coming one step closing to graduating from college debt-free.

Alternatively, at some dorms and off-campus housing facilities, instead of the role of an RA/CA covering the cost 100%, it may instead cover a partial amount. As such, you may only be expected to make a partial or reduced payment to cover your housing cost. As such, this may still be an awesome opportunity if it helps you to work towards of your goal of graduating debt-free.

How can I Find out About RA/CA Positions?

- My recommendation would be for you to call each of the on campus dorms first and inquire if an RA/CA position is open and available.

- Next, after you have contacted the on campus dorms, if no RA/CA Positions are available, contact the off campus dorms to learn if there are any open and available RA/CA Positions.

- When you get an interview, be sure to include your 1) Basic-Ingredients, 2) Four letters of recommendation and 3) a resume. *See Unit Two* on *page 21* to learn more about a *Scholarship Mindset, Required Basic Ingredients, and the Scholarship Non-Negotiables.*

Is there a certain semester in which RA positions may be a little easier to come across?

From my experience in being an RA in college, I have learned that during the summer months when there are less students around, it may be a bit easier to come across an available RA/CA position. My only caution is that if you find a position and accept it, make sure it is a position that will continue to be available to you in both the upcoming *Fall* and *Spring* Semesters.

Is there anything else I need to know about being an RA/CA?

Yes, being an RA/CA either on campus or off campus requires you to be responsible, display leadership abilities, and will challenge your ability to positively communicate with others. Allow me to explain below.

1. <u>Being an RA/CA Requires You to be Responsible</u>

As an RA/CA, you are required to operate in a role that requires a great deal of responsibility. This level of responsibility requires you to act accordingly in the case of an emergency and on behalf of others who will seek you out in the case that they may need help or assistance from a person that represents authority. In the dorm, the RA/CA represents this person of authority to the other students living in the dorm. Because of this, you may have to think fast and be willing to act decisively to assist others in a responsible manner.

2. Being an RA/CA Requires Leadership Skills

In the dorm, there are students at various levels in college. Please, note that if you are in a position of authority as an RA/CA, other students may look up to you. Because of this, please, try to be a positive example so that you lead others in the right direction.

As such, leadership for the RA/CA may often times translate into serving others as a positive voice for others to listen; being a person that aids others as a mentor and role-model that renders guidance and assistance; and is well-known for his/her leadership abilities and good decision-making.

3. Being an RA/CA Requires Positive Communication Skills

Although no one is perfect, as an RA/CA, you may also find yourself in a position in which you are policing your fellow peers and classmates. In this case, be delicate with the way you communicate with them as dorm life vs. outside dorm life may come with its own set of rules. Because of this, I encourage you to communicate in a positive and friendly way with your fellow peers and classmates in a way that would suggest you have a job that you are taking serious as an RA/CA, but you also show respect to your fellow peers and classmates based on the positive and respectful way in which you communicate with them.

4. <u>Being an RA/CA Requires Real Work!</u>

Yes, being an RA/CA gives you status, but no one tells just how much work goes into being a RA/CA. As such, in my role as a college RA/CA, some of the duties we were tasked to do as an RA/CA included walking the dorm at night similar to a security officer; picking up and moving items left at the dorm by other students; completing office and administrative task in the front office; providing tours to parents and potential new students; and completing the labor-intensive task of moving furniture. At the end of the day, in spite of the hard-work, it was worth the free room and board. But, for the record, the role of an RA/CA requires real work that you are expected to complete as a part of the job.

--

I hope you are able to keep this insight in mind to make your role as an RA or CA a pleasant experience for you and others around you. It definitely worked out for me. I hope this chapter from me has been a blessing to you.

Conversation With the Author:
Serving as an RA at Osceola Hall in Tallahassee, Florida

Although it was a lot of work, as a student at FSU, staying off campus at Osceola Hall (500 Chapel Drive in Tallahassee, Florida), I had an amazing experience serving as an RA at Osceola Hall to my amazing college peers and classmates on the *"Might 3 East"* (3rd Floor East Building) and *the New 4 South* (4th Floor South Building). This amazing opportunity covered my housing cost for two (2) years and greatly contributed to my graduate debt-free story.

During my time as an RA, in spite of the work, I was able to make new friends, eat a lot of food, have fun, and use my understanding of the role to share this amazing opportunity with others. To date, I still keep in touch with many of the people I met on my journey as an RA. As I reflect, I am still very grateful and appreciative of the opportunity and experience I had to serve others as an RA at Osceola Hall in Tallahassee, Florida.

Chapter XV

Finding and Applying for Housing Scholarships

Finding and Applying for Housing Scholarships

"Failure is not the worst thing in the world. The very worst is not to try."

Anonymous

Did you know there are scholarships, grants, and beneficial opportunities that will cover your housing expenses for college? While one opportunity may come in the form of a scholarship house, another may come in the form of a grant opportunity that specifically covers the cost of housing. As such, use the information in this chapter to help you find a way to cover the cost of your housing, which will help you to accomplish your goal to graduate from college debt-free.

Also, keep in mind that a housing opportunity or scholarship is anything that will cover the cost of your housing or a portion of it. Because of this, if you receive a partial award (instead of a full payment), this would still be a success as the cost of housing will now be reduced, which could help you to graduate debt-free.

Please, visit our website, www.GraduateDebtFreeClub.com for an updated list of housing scholarships.

Alternatively, please, feel free to search the web for "Housing Scholarships" in your specific city and state. In order to find these scholarships, simply take the following two steps:

Step#1: Open up a search engine and
Step#2: Type in the name of your state and the phrase "housing scholarship" into the search engine.

Using these two step process should lead you to housing scholarships in your specific state. Remember to include the **Mission Possible: Required Basic Ingredients** with every housing scholarship you apply for. *Learn more about the **Mission Possible Required Basic Ingredients in Unit Two on Page 21**.*

Hopefully, the combined housing scholarships you learn about in this unit and other scholarship opportunities in this book will help you accomplish your goal to graduate from college debt-free.

I pray this chapter from me has been a blessing to you.

A Conversation With the Author
My Housing Scholarship with the Southern Scholarship Foundation House

In college, prior to being an RA, one of the scholarships I received was a housing scholarship with the Southern Scholarship Foundation. At the time, it was a great opportunity for me as a new college student because it offered me an incredible reduced amount for room and board for each semester as a part of the scholarship.

Additionally, as one of the tradeoff for the housing scholarship, I was required to complete housing chores, maintain my GPA, and abide by all other rules and guidelines of the scholarship house.

Because the Southern Scholarship Foundation's Housing Scholarship provided me with a great opportunity, I always inform students that if you plan to go to college in the great state of Florida, look into the Southern Scholarship Foundation to apply for the SSF Housing Scholarship.

I hope this information is a blessing to you.

Chapter XVI
Take a College Job That Includes Free Housing

Take a College Job That Includes Free Housing

"Winning is not just about taking chances. It's about having a good attitude despite the outcome."

Dr. J.P. Chisholm

Would you take a job as a college student simply because it includes free housing? In this chapter, I will share three (3) job opportunities that may include free room and board in your area as a benefit to accepting the job opportunity. Please, do your part to read this chapter for understanding, and to research the opportunities in your area prior to applying to confirm if the opportunity in your area offers free housing or a discount on housing as a perk of the job.

Moving forward, the opportunities presented in this chapter will involve us exploring three (3) job opportunities that may provide free housing as a benefit to accepting and working on the job. The opportunities include the following:

- Working in an apartment complex or housing facility as a leasing agent or property agent.

- Working in a 24-hour live in storage facility in the capacity of night security or a night manager.

- Working in the capacity of a live-in caregiver/caretaker.

Some of the above job opportunities with the right level of research may include free housing or a discount on housing. Let's dive in to learn more below.

#1: Working at an Apartment Complex

Although it may not be public knowledge, some apartment complex jobs offer free room and board to employees or a discount on housing for employees. Because housing may be your most expensive bill in college, a job opportunity working at an apartment complex could serve as an opportunity to help you graduate debt-free by providing you with free room and board as a perk of the job or as a discount on housing.

One of the things you may have to give up if you pursue this route is your work-life balance. Since you will work at the place you live, it is likely that your apartment neighbors will know you work for the Apartment Complex and may knock on your door for assistance outside of the work hours.

#2: Working at a 24 Hour Storage Facility

Although it may not be advertised, this is a real opportunity. As such, there are storage facilities that allow its night managers and night security and their families to live on the premises during and after hours in order to promote 24-hour surveillance coverage. To research this opportunity, contact 24 Hour Storage Facilities and others in your area to learn more.

#3: Working in the Capacity of Live-In/Care-giver.

If you have the skills, training, and experience to render assistance to a person in need of a live-in nurse or caregiver's assistant, then this job may be the best alternative for you to have your room and board covered. If you are able to find such an opportunity, I encourage you to have complete transparency concerning your class schedule and unavailability so that you and the person you are caring for are on the same page.

So, next time you are looking for a job opportunity that may include housing benefits as a perk to the job, I am hopeful that you will consider one of the three (3) opportunities referenced in this chapter. I hope you are able to use this information to accomplish your goal of graduating from college debt-free.

Chapter XVII

Buy A Home and Rent it to Friends and Family Members

Buy a Home and Rent it to Friends and Family Members.

"A college home can be a place you live, but also used as a tool to provide for you and your college expenses"

Dr. J.P. Chisholm

Have you ever thought about buying a home to rent to friends or family members and using the money earned to pay for your college tuition, books, and other expenses? If you have thought about this, congratulations on thinking of a creative way to cover the cost of your tuition, books, and other expenses. But, how can we turn this positive thought into a viable opportunity.

In this chapter, my goal is to show you the simple version as to how you can own a home to live in and rent out to others while being a college student. Additionally, I will address the following three (3) keys to help you purchase a home as a college student by addressing the following questions.

1. How can you afford a home as a college student?

2. How to rent it out to friends and/or family members?

3. How can having a home increase your net-worth?

Key#1: How you can afford a home as a college student.

In order to afford a home (while in college), you will need to qualify for a home mortgage. In order to qualify, you will need to have the 4 C's to home buying in order.

C#1: Capacity:

This is important because lenders will want to know your gross income and other financial obligations to determine if you can consistently make mortgage payments. This is determined based on your employment history and how much debt you have vs. how much income you bring in. In order to have this in order, try to maintain consistent employment and make sure your income is more than the debts you have.

C#2: Capital:

Next, capital looks at how much you have been able to save in your bank account and how financially buoyant you are. In order to have this in order, it is recommended that you save enough from your job to have an emergency fund (three to six months) plus enough for a 20% down payment on the home (or its price point) that you are interested in.

C#3: Credit:

Have your credit history together. In order to have this together, it is recommended that you pay all current and past loans, credit cards, and other forms of credit. Also, that you pull your credit report and scores from the credit reporting agencies (Equifax, TransUnion, and Experian) to make sure nothing reflects negatively on your credit history. Banks will look at this information to determine how responsible you will be in paying off a home loan, so make sure your credit information is in order.

C#4: Collateral:

This is how lenders ensure they do not lose money in lending to you. It is often based on the fair value of the home you are interested in purchasing as well as the value of the surrounding homes. The best way to make sure this is in order is to make sure your offer on the home is in line or lower than the bank's appraisal value for the home.

Hopefully, knowing the 4 C's of home ownership will help you understand how you can afford a home as a college student.

Key#2: How to rent it out to friends and family members?

If you decide to rent out your home to friends, family members, or to anyone else interested in renting your home, make sure you get a real lease made by an attorney (to protect your investment) and have it signed by all parties no matter what!

Even if you rent it out to just family members or close friends, have the **renters sign the lease**.

Once you have a lease signed by all parties involved, you are on your way to turning your home into a viable opportunity to covering all your college expenses.

Key#3: How can Having a Home Increase Your Net Worth?

Having a home can (1) increase your *net worth* and (2) bring in revenue.

Having a home increases your net worth because the market value of the house is added to the value of your other personal assets (cash in the bank, investments, and others). Additionally, having a home could add to your income as an investment if you choose to rent it out to a tenant.

Please, find a real estate lawyer, realtor, and banker in your area to get started. I pray this chapter from me has been a blessing to you.

A Conversation With the Author
Three (3) Factors that Discourage People from Purchasing a Home:

1. "I can't afford it!"

Sure, not having enough money is a valid reason to not purchase a home. But this is an easy hurdle to overcome. Moreover, with the amount of federal and private funding programs available at your disposal, you can overcome this hurdle of not having enough money by finding a funding program that works for you. Some available home ownership programs in your community can be contacted by doing the following:

❖ Contacting your local bank or credit union.

❖ Researching home ownership programs via books from your local library, the phonebook, or the internet.

❖ Asking a friend or a family member what they did or who they spoke with in order to get their home.

All of these serve as valuable sources of information that will help you to get over the syndrome of thinking you can't afford a home and walk into your dream of home ownership.

2. It's too Complicated!

Buying a home is just as complicated as renting an apartment. The same elements apply; just different terminology (e.g., lease v. mortgage). Don't allow this to stop you from owning your home! Pick up a book from your local bookstore or library and educate yourself on the process. You will find out that buying a home is just like renting an apartment, but at the end of the paperwork, you are the owner (not the renter).

3. I am Scared.

Fear is not a reason but an excuse and a dangerous weapon that can be used against you. If you are afraid to purchase a home, then your fear could be causing you to miss out on one of the best decisions of your life. Do not allow fear to hold you hostage, instead break away from it and purchase your home as your new place of refuge.

Don't let these three factors discourage you from purchasing your home! Join the club by becoming the homeowner that you would like to be. For more information, learn more at www.GraduateDebtFreeClub.com.

Chapter XVIII

Housing Opportunities
with Friends & Families

Housing Opportunities with Friends and Family Members

"Every door has its own key."

African Proverb

Do you have any family friends or close family members living close to the college you plan on attending? If so, family friends or close family members may open up a housing opportunity for you in either free room and board or a reduced payment to the person in exchange for room and board. This could be a great opportunity to help you accomplish your goal of graduating debt-free.

Also, by choosing to live with friends of the family and/or close family members, it may also offer you additional benefits in the form of home-cooked meals, accountability talks, and trusted people to confide in after having a difficult day. It may also offer you a just-in-case priceless reminder of who you are and what you came to college to accomplish, just-in-case, you encounter something difficult and need a friendly reminder that you can accomplish anything.

So, let's discuss three (3) considerations to help you to embrace this opportunity.

Three (3) Considerations to Help You to Embrace This as a Real Housing Opportunity

#1: Live with people that you trust and respect.

If you have to choose a family friend or a close family member, stay with someone that you trust and respect. This is important because trust and respect are important building blocks to establishing an important foundation. Both of these will help you to trust them and their process even if there is a disagreement with the person or their home rules.

In turn, the person having respect for you may be able to trust you and your decisions (even if they don't understand). Also, there may be less explanation since there is respect for each other and his/her decisions.

Also, please, note that respect is neither toxic, abusive, negative, nor manipulative. If the close friend or family members are showing any of these forms of negativity, then this is likely not the close friend or family members that you would want to stay with.

Prior to moving in with the family friend or close family member, make a decision to abide by the person's rules. This may include rules concerning a curfew, expected chores and responsibilities, relationship policies (or the lack thereof), and even a set bed-time or study time. It may sound strict, but it is a temporary sacrifice to accomplish your goals of graduating from college debt-free.

#2: It Gives You a Home Away from Home

Next, keep in mind that although this person may not know you personally, this person may be a person that knows of you, your family, or your family's reputation. Because of this, this person may go above and beyond to make you feel welcomed and that you are in a comfortable environment.

Additionally, the person may see you in a similar way that your parents see you. Because of this, there may be a lot of grace and understanding if you ever get something wrong or there is a misunderstanding, which is something that we all need. Hopefully, you will also show them grace and understanding as well.

Ultimately, this housing opportunity may start to feel similar to your experience at home. Or you may come to the conclusion that you are in a positive environment you can consider your home away from home. I personally would find this to be a positive outcome.

#3: Be useful, not just a user!

Also, just like staying there benefits you, try to occasionally do something for the family friend or family member that you are living with to show appreciation to the person. For example, offer to make the person food, pay for a special dinner, baby-sit, take out the trash, pet-sit, or help their child with homework. Just try to be a blessing to the person just like the opportunity of living there is a blessing to you.

I hope this chapter from me has been a blessing to you.

A Conversation With the Author:
Making the Sacrifice

Sometimes, in order to hold on to the right move and ultimately end up where we would like to be, it's important that we learn to put our ego aside. Make the sacrifice by checking your attitude at the door and having the conversation with your folks. Ask them the question, "Is it ok for me to continue living here free while in college?" If they say, "Yes!" then you have made a big step in saving money from rent that will help you accomplish your goal to graduate debt-free.

I pray this information has been a blessing to you.

Chapter XIX

Go to College Close to Home

Go to College Close to Home

"Winning is not just about taking chances. It's about having a good attitude despite the outcome."
Dr. J.P. Chisholm

Would it really be that terrible for you to stay at home while attending a college close to home? In this chapter, I will share nine advantages of attending a college close to home.

Nine (9) Nifty Reasons to Attend College Close to Home

1) Save money on rent.

2) Be showered with love from parent(s)/guardians.

3) Enjoy an occasional home-cooked meal!

4) Have a parent or family member to confide in after having a difficult day.

5) You don't have to worry about moving out to a new place or buying new furniture.

6) For your college years, you can chant the phrase, "there's no place like home!"

7) Go to college close to home and stay at home

8) Use the time to build up your credit.

9) It will help you to graduate from college debt-free.

Although there are several factors that could influence your decision to go to college close to home and stay at home, the bottom line comes down to one simple question: **will this option work for you?** If the answer is in the affirmative, then note that staying at home is a real option that can and will help you to save money so you can accomplish your goal to graduate from college debt-free.

I hope this chapter from me has been a blessing to you.

Conversation With the Author:
I know credit cards are bad, but I am getting one anyway.

There are always some people that admit that they understand that credit cards are usually bad and yet, they choose to get it anyway. To any such group, I do not recommend getting a credit card. But I do recognize that for some, this may be the only option in cases of an emergency. Here's a conversation that may help you to make the right credit card decision. It features 8 solid suggestions to cover you and prevent you from making a terrible credit card decision. Here are 8 factors to thoroughly consider before signing up for a credit card for emergencies:

1. Read through your credit card material: No matter how boring your credit card information may seem, ensure you read through. If you do not understand, ask questions. Remember, it's better to be safe than sorry.

2. Call their customer service number and assess how helpful they are. How long were you on hold? Were they very accessible or was it difficult to reach a person? How flexible are they with bill payments—must it be received in the mail on the date of or will they accept

payments via the phone or online? Are there any fees for payment? Yes, sometimes, credit companies charge you a fee to pay your bill if you are not paying it a certain way.

3. Only use it in cases of emergency.

4. Try to get one with a low-interest rate with a fixed amount.

5. Always shop around for the lowest interest rate.

6. Please, read through the fine print to confirm if your interest rate is fixed or variable. Some credit cards start off as fixed and later change into a variable interest rate either after the first year or based on spending habits. So, ensure you read through your credit card material to know when these shifts will affect you.

7. Pay your credit card bill before interest begins to accrue.

I pray this insight from me has been a blessing to you.

Unit Five:
Mission Possible: Covering the Cost of Books

Chapter XX

Ways to Cover the Cost for College Books

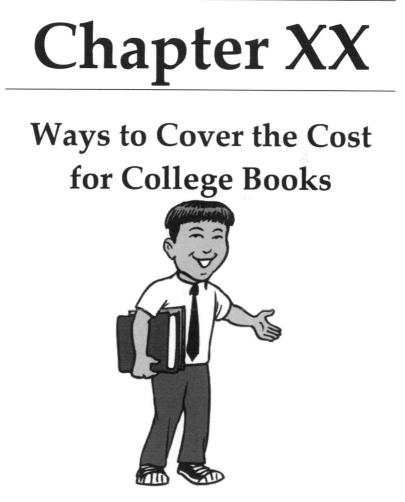

Ways to Cover the Cost for College Books

"Ideas are funny little things. They don't work unless you do."

Anonymous

Need books for school? I am sure you do because having books in college can be a mandatory necessity to pass a course. However, books can be very expensive. In this chapter, I will share a few easy to do, 100% legal tips that will save you money and take you a step closer to achieving your goal of graduating debt-free.

Here are three (3) simple strategies to get books for college without paying an arm and a leg.

Strategy#1: Use the library.

Sometimes, college students overlook the resourcefulness of campus libraries, as well as the local libraries in their city. Sometimes, these local hubs of knowledge are so resourceful you may find the exact book your professor is using in a course. Hopefully, the lesson you take from this point is that before purchasing an expensive book for class, try checking for it at both your college's library and local city library.

Strategy #2: Search online for the e-book copy.

Although it may be surprising to some, I have found several books used in class published online (with permission from the Author and/or Publisher) as a free downloadable e-book.

In order to find these books, I will sometimes search for the name of the book in popular online search engines.

Before downloading any book online, be sure to check that the author of the book or his/her publishing company has consented to a free download of the book. Sometimes this information from the author or the publishing company is posted on the very page you are downloading the book from.

Please, feel free to research and learn more about authors and publishers that allow online downloads of their books.

Strategy #3: Rent the book.

If you are still having a hard time finding the book for your class, in exchange for a small fee, try to rent the book online from an e-book company or rental company. Below are two websites that allow you rent e-books:

https://www.lendle.me/

https://www.booklending.com/

Finding your books and not spending an arm or a leg for it always feels like finding gold. I hope the information in this chapter helps you find the books you need for your courses.

I pray this information from me has been a blessing to you.

Chapter XXI

Take Action by Asking for the Books

Take Action by Asking for the Books

"Even though you know a thousand things, ask the person who knows one." – Turkish Proverb

If you still don't have the books, whom can you ask for the books? Try asking your professor or course lecturer if he or she has a copy of the book(s) that can be loaned to you. Alternatively, use social media to post about the book by simply inquiring if anyone has the book. Like magic, asking the right person may make the books appear. Let me explain.

I have learned there are a lot of people that will help you with anything you are working on if you are willing to ask for help. Now, this is not a perfect system and of course there will be individuals that are not interested in helping, but I believe you are more likely to find success in asking for help, than failure.

Below, I will share three (3) pivotal groups that can help you get the books you need for class.

#1: Ask Your Professors

As a college student I learned that sometimes the Professor has extra copies of the book that he/she may be willing to loan you as a student in their class. Interestingly, the only way to learn about this is by inquiring from the Professor. In order to do this, I would recommend that you either enquire from the Professor after class or you schedule a time to discuss this with the Professor during their office hours.

If the Professor is unavailable or you cannot meet up, try sending the Professor a professional email inquiring if he/she has a copy of the class book that you could borrow from him/her. Please, remember to be both polite and respectful at all times when dealing with your instructor (even if you do not feel it is reciprocated).

#2: Ask Your College Friends That Have Already Taken the Class

As a rule of thumb, I have learned that college students, roommates, and friends will share books with someone they know if you are willing to ask them. Especially, if the other person with the books have already taken the course and are no longer using the books. As such, this creates an opportunity to get the books you need to accomplish your goal.

In order to make this happen, I believe you should reach-out to other college students, your roommates, and friends concerning, 1) if anyone has the books you need and 2) if the person would be willing to share them with you for this semester.

#3: Make a Post on Social Media to get the Books

Use your social media platform to get the books you need. In order for this to work, simply post on your wall a question like "Does anyone have the specific books you need for (name the course)?" In doing so, a friend may reply to you via social media that they have the books you need.

Alternatively, after posting on social media, don't be surprised if someone sees your post and shares it with others that may lead to someone you don't know seeing the post and responding by giving you the books you need.

I hope you are able to use this information to get the books you need and get closer to your goal of graduating from college debt-free.

A Conversation With the Author
In Memory of an Incredible Teacher,
Ms. Linda Ghanayem
(2/28/1953 – 4/24/2017)

One of my favorite teachers, Ms. Linda Ghanayem told me something that really sparked my interest in reading. She said that authors hide things in books that only a selected group of people are supposed to know. As a curious kid that wanted to know everything, this statement made me want to read every book I could get my hands on in order to find this special information for the selected few.

As an adult, I know Ms. Linda Ghanayem just wanted me to read more and she just knew what to say to peak my interest. Like a seed planted in a fertile soil, her words and positive affirmations about reading have grown me into the avid reader and writer that I am today. I appreciate her for sparking my interest.

To date, I still have a zeal for reading and the knowledge that you gain through it. I hope this information from me encourages you to find one book that speaks to you so that you start reading everything just like I did. And not just reading for school, but for personal enrichment. Through your reading, you can travel and explore countries around the world; learn about careers and job opportunities; and gain experience and confidence through reading to not only explore your ideas but research ways to bring them into fruition. Ultimately, this was the fire that came from the spark Ms. Linda Ghanayem initiated.

Hopefully, I have sparked your interest to read more for yourself just like Ms. Linda Ghanayem did for me (and not just for school). I am excited about your future and through your reading, writing, and studying, who you will become.

I pray this chapter from me has been a blessing to you.

Chapter XXII

Using Bartering As a Strategy for Books

Using Bartering As A Strategy for Books

"If you aim at nothing, you'll hit it every time."
Anonymous

Did you know that you could use bartering to get books instead of spending money on books? How does that make sense? Because bartering has value. It allows you to exchange something of value to another person for something of value to you. This could be a useful strategy to add to your graduate debt-free arsenal as it will allow you to trade something of value in exchange for the books that you need (instead of spending money on new or used books), which will help you to graduate debt-free.

What Does It mean to barter?

When you barter, you are negotiating the exchange of goods or services for other goods or services without using or referencing money as the medium of exchange.

How can I start to barter for books?

You can start bartering for books by reaching out to four (4) groups:

Four (4) Groups that May Be Open to a Book Barter Arrangement

o Group#1: Reach out to friends.

o Group#2: Reach out to other college students that you may have met on your college campus, in class, and/or at your dorm.

o Group#3: Reach out to other college students that are involved in the same organizations that you are involved in.

o Group#4: Reach out to others using Social Media.

Also, remember safety when bartering by agreeing to meet in very public, well-lit spots on campus where there are a lot of people and a lot of cameras. It may also be a good idea to take a friend with you to make sure that you are not by yourself since it is believed that there is safety in numbers.

What if someone wants to meet-up off campus to barter?

If someone wants to meet up with you off-campus to barter, here are seven (7) tips that will help you to safely barter with the person.

Seven (7) Tips that will Help You to Safely Barter with the Person that Wants to Meet-Up Off-Campus

Anytime you barter, **always make sure that your safety is your first priority** by always bartering from a safe distance. This could be achieved by following these safety precautions:

- ❑ #1: Try using the mail whenever you can to complete your bartering transactions.

- ❑ #2: Never give out your personal home address, dorm room, and/or dorm location. Instead, use a P.O. Box address provided through the local post office or your college. Use this address as the mailing address for the person to mail you the books, which upon receiving you will promptly mail the books to the person.

- ❑ #3: Never allow or agree to meet a complete stranger at your home or meet them at their home. Instead, always meet at a central location that is highly populated (e.g., shopping mall, inside a gym, at a very public place on campus, inside your church, or at a local restaurant or café that you are familiar with). Also, make sure the area that you decide to meet is both well-lit and is being monitored by camera.

- #4: And if you do meet at one of the aforementioned places mentioned in #3, always take a buddy along with you to further ensure your safety instead of going alone.

- #5: In addition, have mobile accountability partners (like a friend, fraternity/sorority brother or sister, sibling, parent, grandparent, best friend, spouse) that you know very well and they know you that will call you at a specified time to confirm that the barter went well and that you are safe. The mobile accountability person (unlike the buddy) is not physically with you and as a result should know the specifics of who/what/when/where/ and why you are meeting with the person you plan to barter with. Also, if the accountability partner cannot reach you at the agreed upon time, they are already on notice that they need to promptly report the details of your bartering incident to the police and/or other authority. This type of accountability further ensures your safety is of top priority.

- #6: Remember, you only bartering for books to use in class. As such, don't get tricked into agreeing to perform personal services in exchange for books that could dangerously place you inside the person's home. Because of this, some examples of personal services that I would <u>never</u> agree to do would include babysitting, dog-sitting, private massages, washing the person's clothes in their home, cleaning the person's home/house, and others that would place me inside *a stranger's* private home or offer services that would reveal your private residence's address to a *stranger*. Instead, have them meet you in a central location as mentioned in #3. Also, be sure to have a buddy along with you and your accountability partner on standby.

❑ #7: Check local laws in your area to make sure that bartering is legal in your area.

Furthermore, by making safety your first concern, having levels of accountability, and knowing the law in your specific area concerning bartering, you are free to explore this option at your discretion. But please remember to be careful as bartering is not for everyone and could be dangerous. For more information on this topic, please feel free to learn more from our website: www.GraduateDebtFreeClub.com.

I hope this Chapter for me has been a blessing to you!

A Conversation With the Author:
Bartering 101 for College Students

In college, learn to barter everything! It can be a very effective means to save money and get you the things you want as a college student. Usually, in college towns (or smaller communities of people), there is an abundance of intelligent and talented people that will eagerly barter with you in exchange for something they may want from you. It was in such an environment that I bartered to have one of my first business websites and business materials created in exchange for me agreeing to refer clients to a web designer's new business.

After our bartering, we both walked away feeling like winners as I got what I wanted and the person got what they wanted. I am very thankful for having this experience. It taught me the importance and power of using bartering to get what you want instead of using cash.

I pray this chapter of my life is able to add a blessing unto yours.

Unit Six:
Other Ways To Pay For College (Tuition, Housing, and Books)

Chapter XXIII

Other Practical Ways to Free Up Money for College

Other Practical Ways To Free Up Money For College

"… Help doesn't always have to be in the form of a hero saving the day, but doing what you can, how you can."

Dr. J.P. Chisholm

Have you ever thought about what real expenses you could cut out from your monthly bills and rechannel to your college expenses? If so, this chapter will give you some practical ideas concerning slight financial shifts and adjustments that can be used in funding your college expenses.

Moreover, I have learned help doesn't always have to be in the form of a hero saving the day, but doing what you can, how you can. For some, the route to pay for college expenses will come in the form of scholarship, awards, and other beneficial opportunities. But for others, it may come from trying to find practical ways to free up money and save for it. As such, this chapter shares practical tips and strategies on how to cut your monthly expenses, and use the amount saved to cover tuition fees, college books, and college housing expenses.

As a first step for this chapter, if you have not already done so, it is recommended that you open a savings bank account exclusively for tuition fees, books, and housing expenses. All money that you free up should be added or transferred to this account. Please, check out our website: www.GraduateDebtFreeClub.com to learn more.

What are some helpful tips you could use to cut monthly expenses and rechannel towards funding your college expenses?

Below are nine helpful tips to help cut down your monthly expenses.

#1: Review Payment Plans.

Don't just blindly pay bills because you receive them in the mail. Request itemized statements of the charges and double check to make sure you are not paying for something that is already paid off. In today's automated society, accounts get mixed up and you might accidentally be charged for someone else's debt. Make sure you are paying what rightfully belongs to you. Excess funds should not be misapplied, but put away in your exclusive personal savings account for the sole purpose of saving for college expenses.

#2: Use Coupons and Online Discount Codes When Shopping

Coupons and Online Discount Codes can save you tons of money and they are easy to get. In order to find coupons and discount codes, all you need to do is check the printed and online newspapers, printed and online advertisements, websites that feature discount codes and/or coupons.

Additionally, coupons may be found in your physical mailbox as companies still share promotional material through the mail and discount codes may be found in your email after signing up for an online newsletter that offers an online discount code for joining. Use the coupons and discount codes to save money! Please, keep in mind that what you save can be applied to your exclusive personal savings account you are using for the sole purpose of saving for college expenses.

.

#3: Shop at Discount Stores

Change your shopping habits and start shopping at discount stores to save money. Often times, these discount stores and websites have all the same items but at a discounted rate. All money saved can be added to your exclusive personal savings account.

#4: Create a Physical or Digital Receipt Wall

On this wall, you attach all your weekly bills and receipts to find out where your money is going. You will be amazed by all of the things and places that your money goes toward but you never even realize because it was not on the radar. When you are able to cut things out, add what you are saving to your exclusive personal savings account that you are using for the sole purpose of saving for college expenses.

#5: Buy Used Cars

New cars depreciate (lose value) the moment you drive them off the car dealership lot. Because of this, learn to set a car budget that you will not exceed, research deals, and buy used cars in good condition that you can purchase with cash or pay off quickly. Please, note that not having a monthly car note will free up a substantial amount of funds each month that you can repurpose.

Also, consider buying vehicles from family members, estate sales, rental car companies, repossession sales, and others that will allow you to buy the car at a discount. In doing so, always have the vehicle inspected by a certified mechanic you trust so that you can properly assess the value and true costs of any repairs needed.

Additionally, before you purchase, confirm the value of the vehicle by referencing one of the popular car guide books or online sites that features the value of various vehicles. Use this vehicle reference guide as a gage to understand how much of a deal you are getting in purchasing the vehicle from the vender you decide to purchase from. Add the saved difference to your exclusive savings account.

#6: Eliminate Credit Card Debts

You will be amazed at how much of your monthly income you will be able to keep in your pocket if you eliminate credit card debt(s) and only purchase what you can pay for with cash. The interest rates on credit continually consume your money especially if you are only making the minimum payments. Aggressively paying off the cards will give you freedom and free up your funds to do other things. Add what you save to your exclusive personal savings account.

#7: Don't keep excess cash in your pocket

The more you have in your pocket, purse, or money just sitting in your car, the more likely you will spend it that day. Therefore, put your money in a less conspicuous place than your pocket, purse, or car, which will save you from spending it. A good place to keep your excess money is in your exclusive personal savings account that you are using for the sole purpose of saving for college expenses.

#8: Reduce your Digital TV Subscriptions, Cable Bills, Satellite Bills, and any other TV Subscriptions

Companies win by selling you TV and Station Subscriptions, Cable TV, and/or Satellite TV with access to tons of movies, television programs, and others. Instead of paying for access to all of this programs, reduce your TV, cable, and satellite subscriptions. This can be especially easy if you are paying for stuff you don't really watch.

Also, much of the programs and movies can be watched online via websites that freely and legally screen digital content. Alternatively, TV series and movies can also be purchased by paying a one-time fee and maintained digitally for you to watch at your convenience. You can also gain access to programming and movies by checking out this type of material at your local public library or college campus library.

Additionally, special shows are often featured on YouTube.com and other digital screening services. Or, you can always meet at a friend's house to watch your favorite movies and TV shows.

Since there are so many options available, try reducing some of the ones you have, and add what you save to your exclusive personal account.

#9: Reduce Monthly Magazine Subscriptions

Some public libraries subscribe to local and national magazine publications and keep copies within their collections. Make a regular visit to the library to read your favorite publications, instead of a paying a subscription. This will help reduce your monthly spending budget, and you can add what you save to your exclusive savings account.

--

Here is some final advice for both parents and students in high-school or college.

For Parents:

The tips shared in this chapter are easy to start and can be implemented in your day-to-day routine while your college dreamer is just a baby. Remember, the more time you have, the more money you are able to save toward college expenses or add to their exclusive personal savings account.

For High-School Students and College Students

As a final word of advice, use the information in this chapter to save what you can within the limited window of time you have to do so.

I pray this chapter from me has been a blessing to you.

A Conversation With the Author:
Tired of Receiving Junk Credit Card Mail?

What's in your mail? I am guessing it's the same thing in mine—an overabundance of annoying credit card, insurance, and other documents with all my personal information on it. This type of mail is not innocent because once you receive it, if you do not completely shred it up, it could lead to someone getting your precious information and stealing your identify (identity theft). But there is a solution to this annoying mail madness and the great news is that it only takes less than two minutes to completely deactivate the mail madness and other mail solicitation for five years. It's simple. All you do is call the following number and by doing so, you are choosing to stop receiving the thousands of offers from credit cards and other companies. Here's the number: 1-888-567-8688. Enjoy!

Now that I have done it, I am excited about opening the mailbox and not receiving tons of solicitations. I hope this chapter from me has been a blessing to you.

Chapter XXIV

Make A Deal with the Parents

Make a Deal With the Parents

"Positive thoughts. Positive results ."
Mrs. Alnora Chisholm (Mom)

Have you ever thought of making a deal with your parents/guardians to pay for college expenses? By agreeing to discuss the financial plan, expenses, what the parents/ guardians, as well as what you can do, you will be alleviating a great deal of stress on all sides. To do this successfully, there will have to be openness on all sides and a willingness to listen and understand, which admittedly can be difficult at times between a parent and an aspiring college student. But if the sides can work through their disputes, it may be mutually beneficially to all parties involved.

So, let's agree on some ground rules prior to having this important discussion.

Ten Ground Rules to Help You Kick Start College Plan Discussion.

1. Agree to discuss the financial plan for college.

Pick an afternoon when all parties are free. Turn off your phones and other interruptions and select a quiet and confidential environment (e.g., your living room) since you will be discussing college and the money to pay for it.

2. Set Ground Rules.

Setting ground rules is very important because these are the rules you will use to discuss college and the money to pay for it.

In establishing ground rules, it's important you both agree **not** to throw one another's short falls or mistakes at each other. However, you may address a particular situation in a neutral manner as long as you are not making it about the other person or using it for   personal   attack.

Also, let's agree to <u>not</u> use curse words, name calling, or other derogatory language towards one another through the course of the discussion since this can quickly turn a respectful and peaceful discussion into a yelling match or worse.

Lastly, you must all agree that if one party does not agree with the other party, they are still okay. This is the famous "we will still love each other even if we agree to disagree" rule, which is an important rule to keep families together even if family members see things differently.

3. Find out the Concerns of Both Parties.

Give a sheet of paper to each person present. Have each side draft all their concerns on one side of the paper.

4. Find out the Short-term and Long-term Goals of Both Parties.

Then, without seeing the other person's concerns, on the back of the same paper, individually list the goals you would like to see accomplished in the order of priority within the following time frames:

Short-term Goals

Short-term goals are goals you would like to accomplish within a year to five years. For example, paying for your semester of college or getting a job to pay for tuition.

Long-term Goals

Long-term goals are goals that you would like to see accomplished over the next five to ten plus years.

5. Share your individual concerns and goals with the other person.

Compare your list of goals with the other person. Listen intently to each other without interrupting. Ask questions (without attacking) in order to get a better understanding of the significance of the items listed

6. Determine if you both have mutual goals.

Take your time and review the short term and long term goals that each of you articulated. After careful review, determine if both parties have any mutual goals they can both agree to work on together.

7. Share Your Sources of Income (if any) and Expenses (if any).

Share your income sources and expenses with the other person and use it to make a budget. Please, note that clear communication is about transparency. As such, both parties will have to work to make a deal and you want the other person to understand that the parties will need to work together in order to make this work. Be sure to be honest and put *all of your cards* on the table.

8. Agree to Draft a Monthly Budget Together.

Parents and student must agree to draft a monthly budget together using what they have with the understanding that excess funds between the parties could be used in covering some of your college expenses like tuition and books.

Also, this budget may become the plan of action to help the parties achieve their goals. Ensure you factor in funds for unexpected emergencies, to keep each other accountable.

9. Follow-up.

Schedule a follow up meeting to revisit the plan at the end of each month to find out how well you were able to stick with it and determine ways to improve for the next month.

10. Celebrate your accomplishments!

Find low budget ways of celebrating both baby-steps and milestones.

--

Now that we have the ground rules out of the way, what do we discuss next?

What do we Discuss Next After the Ground Rules?

After the ground rules have been addressed, what are some important subjects that either current college student or future college student, and parents/guardians need to discuss:

o Can parents offer financial support to future college student so college student can graduate debt-free (or as close to debt-free as possible)?

o Will future college student or current college student continue to abide by certain parents' rules while parents are offering support to college student? And what will this look like?

o Living arrangements for a college student staying at home. *If this is a topic that needs to be discussed, please, read or revisit* **Chapter 19: "Go to College Close to Home."**

o Freeing up money for college expenses. . *If this is a topic that needs to be discussed, please read or revisit* **Chapter 23: "Other Practical Ways to Pay for College."**

What if my Parent(s)/Guardian(s) Cannot Help With College?

It is absolutely okay if your parent(s)/guardian(s) cannot help you pay for college. Please, continue to appreciate them and be thankful for what they have done to help you get this far.

Also, the good news is that you are currently reading, *"How to Graduate From College Debt-Free"* for solutions. As such, you should be able to learn some strategies to help yourself.

So, stay positive and believe everything is going to work-out.

I pray this chapter has been a blessing to you.

A Conversation With the Author:
No Person is an Island

Sometimes, great people become great because they have the help of others. There is no shame in receiving help to achieve your goals. So, don't feel ashamed if you need help. Just ask for it, accept it, and use the support you receive to accomplish your goals.

But, there is one important thing I would like to point-out. Although there is no shame in needing help and asking for it, there is shame in one scenario:

Needing help, but being too proud to ask for it.

Hopefully, that doesn't apply to you. But if it does, seek out the support you need to accomplish your goals. I pray this chapter from me has been a blessing to you.

Unit Seven:
Mission Possible:
You Now Have the Tools to Graduate From College Debt-Free

Chapter XXV

Commencement

Commencement

"If you are afraid of your ideas, you are afraid of yourself!"

Dr. J.P. Chisholm

Who are the members of your tribe? And what can you use their encouragement to accomplish? Well, who you keep around you in your inner circle is important because they become the people that will influence you, push you, and help you to be all that you can be.

Some of the members of my tribe were my late parents, Mr. Eugene & Mrs. Alnora Chisholm. They influenced me, pushed me, and helped me to be all that I can be. They were able to do this by equipping me with the tools needed to believe in myself, to believe in my talents, and to always believe there is a bright future ahead of me. These positive beliefs were instilled in me as a child and etched in my heart from their words of encouragement and positive affirmations; as Mom would say, "Positive thoughts! Positive results!" and my dad reassuring me that "I can do this! You already got it!" Today, although they are no longer here, I fondly hold on to the warm memories as they live on in my heart.

Another important tribe member would be the teachers that inspired me to learn new things and opened up my mind to the vastness of the world through Literature, Science, History, Art, and Math.

It was Mrs. Oz Zilahy, one of my former high-school English Teachers that taught me the power of perspective. In doing so, Mrs. Zilahy would emphasize the impact of *choice* and how our individualized choices in selecting to see the world from an optimistic point of view or a pessimistic point of view could determine if life's adversity would stop you or motivate you to keep going. From that lesson, I chose optimism and I continue to do so even to this day, so I can continue to learn the bigger lessons from life and use them to motivate myself in spite of any mountain or obstacle I have to overcome. To Mrs. Oz. Zilahy, former English Teacher at Jean Ribault Senior High School in Jacksonville, Florida and to every other teacher that both inspired and enlightened me, thank you for what you did and for being a part of my tribe.

I also believe my Pastors and church family would be members of my tribe because the good Lord used them in a mighty way to instill hope and faith in me and in knowing that all things will work together for my good. Additionally, one of the greatest principles I learned from my Pastors and church family is that *my hands are small* and because of that they will <u>never</u> be able to handle all the stress, drama, heart-break, pain, and stuff that happens to me.

But, God's hands are so much bigger than mine and I can always put my concerns, worries, and things I can't handle in the hands of a Godly Father, Godly Protector, and Godly Provider so that I am able to keep moving forward with a positive attitude when things go haywire.

My last tribe member has been in my corner since we met at a leadership conference in Tallahassee, Florida. We started off as friends, then to a dating relationship, and for the last fifteen years and counting, we have been husband and wife. Through our love, we help and support each other to accomplish goals, to raise our family, and to motivate each other to be the best version of ourselves.

Collectively, my tribe keeps me positive, strong, and encouraged. Through their positive affirmations, warm memories, life lessons, love and support, I continue to evolve into the best version of myself. And to this end, I truly appreciate the impact and influence that my tribe has had on my life.

But I am not the only one with a tribe. You too may have a tribe that believes in you, what you will become, and what you will accomplish. Tap into your tribe! These trustworthy individuals will keep you encouraged and help you become more than you ever thought possible.

Moreover, I look forward to the day that I too can learn more of your story. Keep me in the loop via our   website: www.GraduateDebtFreeClub.com.

I pray this chapter from me has been a blessing to you!

A Conversation With the Author:
Find Your Goldmine and Stick With it.

Looking for a goldmine to help you pay for your tuition? Just find something that works for you and stick with it. Because as you have now read, there are several opportunities available for you concerning college tuition, housing, books, and more. So, try to make this work for you by trying different strategies from Mission Possible: How to Graduate From College Debt Free.

In doing so, this will help you find your goldmine, which are the strategies that will work for you and help you graduate debt-free. I pray this book from me has been able to be a blessing to you. Please, continue to connect with us at www.GraduateDebtFreeClub.com.

Congratulations!
Now Apply It!

Glossary

Bartering: *Exchanging one good or service for another.*

Black: *When you have money left over (more revenues than expenses), you are considered in the black, which means you are technically in a healthy financial position.*

College Saving Account: *A Savings Account opened up with a bank, credit union, or other financial institution used exclusively for saving for college and spending on college expenses.*

Credit Report: *A compiled report that includes information such as your bill payment history, if you have ever been arrested, sued or filed bankruptcy.*

Emergency funds: *Emergency funds usually refer to at least 3-5 months of income saved or invested conservatively based on your immediate bills and life expenses for emergency use only.*

Financial discipline: *This refers to setting a financial goal (i.e. $10,000 dollars saved per year) and putting the time, energy, and resources towards achieving your goal.*

Financial Stewardship: *This means keeping track of your money by knowing where it is going.*

Interest Payments: *Money gained on an investment by way of interest.*

Launch Party: *A type of celebration that previews a new idea, book, business, or other similar novelty and brings in additional money for the project.*

Long Term Investment: *An investment that is held for over 10 years.*

Networks: *Dependable personal, business, or organizational contacts that you can rely on.*

Net Worth: *A person's net worth is the total value a person has when all their possessions are calculated such as a home and various other investments like the ones* mentioned in *How to Make Your Past, a Blessing To Your Future* minus all the person's debt including the person's mortgage, any unpaid credit card balances, etc. Total Assets minus total liabilities of an individual or company.

Private Mortgage Insurance: Extra insurance that many lenders require from buyers who make less than a 20% down payment when buying a house in order to protect the lender in the event that the buyer defaults (doesn't pay) the loan. You can usually cancel it once you have paid your mortgage down to the point that it equals 80 percent of the original purchase price or the appraisal value of your home at the time the loan was obtained (whichever is less).

Red: A term of art that refers to technically being in a very dangerous financial place where your expenses exceed your income.

Residual income: This refers to steady sources of income you can count on to determine how much money you actually make. All forms of compensation received on your payday are considered a portion of what makes up your residual income. Your total residual income is the total amount of money you actually receive over a year's time.

Short-term goals: Are goals that you would like to accomplish within a year up to five years. For example, fixing the plumbing, planning a summer vacation, paying for your semester of college, saving 10% of income.

X-Factors: *God-given gifts and creative talents that can be used to earn additional money.*

Learn More at:
www.GraduateDebtFreeClub.com
www.Investitude.com
www.YoungInvestors.org
www.JuanChisholm.com